Health, Hygiene, and Nutrition

Grades 3–4

by
Deirdre Englehart

Published by Instructional Fair
an imprint of
Frank Schaffer Publications®

Instructional Fair

Author: Deirdre Englehart
Editor: Cary Malaski
Interior Designer: Jannette Bole

Frank Schaffer Publications®

Instructional Fair is an imprint of Frank Schaffer Publications.

Send all inquiries to:
Frank Schaffer Publications
8720 Orion Place
Columbus, Ohio 43240-2111

Health, Hygiene, and Nutrition—Grades 3-4

ISBN: 0-7424-2757-9

6 7 8 9 10 PAT 09

Table of Contents

Introduction 4
KWL Chart. 5
My Personal Timeline. 6
Sharing My Timeline 7
How Healthy Are You? 8
Healthy People Scavenger Hunt. 9
Guess Who? 10

Nutrition
Your Nutrition 11
My Food Pyramid 12
The Five Food Friends—
 Readers' Theater 13–14
My Diet 15
How Much Is a Serving? 16
Nutrition Labels 17
Facts from the Bread Group 18
A Breakfast to See Me Through
 the Morning 19
Cereal Choices 20
Starch Test 21
Facts from the Vegetable Group 22
Cooked versus Raw 23
Facts from the Fruit Group 24
Fruit Juice Fun 25
Use Your Senses 26
Facts from the Dairy Group 27
Checking Out Calcium 28
Milk Confusion 29
Facts from the Protein Group 30
Digestive Discoveries 31
Breaking Down Digestion. 32
Facts from the Fat Group. 33
French Fry Fat Test 34
Sweet as Can Be. 35
Sugar by Any Other Name 36
Regular versus Low-Fat. 37
Roll for Your Food 38
The Best Selection 39
Healthy Creation Contest 40
Fast-Food Frenzy 41
Create Your Own Restaurant 42
Favorite Foods Data 43
Healthy America? 44
Nutrition Review. 45

General Health
Your Health 46
Germaine's Travels 47
Your Body's Defenses 48
They're in Your Blood 49
Germs Multiply. 50
Catch a Germ 51
Hand-Washing Habits 52
Rate the Hand Washing 53
School Illnesses 54
Hand-Washing Comic Strip 55
Cold Control 56
Let's Grow Bacteria 57
The Big Sneeze. 58
A Germ Story 59
An A-Peeling Skin 60
Skin Cells 61
Antibiotic Scientist. 62
General Health Review 63

Dental Hygiene
Your Dental Hygiene. 64
Visiting Dr. Bicuspid 65
Brush Away the Plaque 66
My Pearly Whites 67
Homemade Toothpaste. 68
Toothpaste Ads 69
A Mouth Full of Teeth 70
Soaperman 71
Dental Hygiene Review 72

Physical and Mental Health
Your Physical Health 73
Cardiovascular Creations 74
Stretching. 75
Intensity of Exercise 76
Taking Your Heart Rate 77
The Flexibility Test. 78
The Strength Test 79
Repetitions Graphing 80
ABC Fitness Fun 81
Fitness Charades 82
Name the Game. 83
Ask the Expert 84
My Favorite Exercise 85
Physical Fitness Review 86

Exercising Your Mind 87
An Ideal Friend 88
The Stress Factor 89
The Pressure Is On 90
Coping with Situations at School 91
Mental Health Review 92

Safety
Keeping Yourself Safe 93
Just Avoid It 94
Looks Can Be Deceiving 95
Fuel for the Fire 96
Fire Extinguisher 97
First Aid Kits 98
Safety Situations 99
Food Safety 100
Just Chill 101
Home Safety Assessment 102
A Poster for Safety 103
A True Safety Story 104
Choices and Consequences 105
Smoking 106
Take a Deep Breath 107
The Effects of Smoking 108

Do You Smell Smoke? 109
Alcohol Is Addictive 110
Drunk Driving Simulation 111
The Cycle of Addiction 112
Magazine Messages 113
Safety Review 114

Review
They All Matter 115
Still Wondering 116
Give One, Get One 117
Healthy Acrostic Poem 118
Feed Yourself Well 119
Destination: Digestive System 120
A Scrambled Story 121
A Haiku by You 122
Peer Pressure Readers' Theater 123
Connections to Standards 124
Suggested Books for Health, Hygiene,
   and Nutrition 125
Healthy You Award 126

Answer Key 127–128

Introduction

Growth and development depend on good nutrition, exercise, cleanliness, and the ability to keep ourselves safe from harm. Establishing good habits at an early age in all of these areas that affect health will help ensure a healthy body, mind, and attitude.

Good nutrition is the backbone of a healthy body. Foods from the various food groups provide our bodies with the nutrients, vitamins, and minerals needed to grow and function. The food pyramid helps us plan how much of certain foods to eat to ensure that we are eating healthfully.

Exercise helps us feel and look good, and it helps strengthen muscles and bones as we grow. Children should exercise daily for about an hour. This can take the form of sports, outdoor play, recess, bike riding, and so much more.

Proper hygiene keeps our bodies clean and safe from harmful germs. Germs can cause sickness and tooth decay. Hand-washing is the best defense against germs and illnesses, along with knowing how to avoid unhealthy situations.

Knowing how to stay safe also helps keep us healthy. We can stay safe by following rules at school and at home, by making good choices, and by thinking about the consequences of our actions. It is important for children to know that they control their actions and that they should try to make good decisions.

This book covers all areas of health, hygiene, and nutrition and is a practical book to add to your curriculum. It will teach your students a lot about their bodies and how best to care for themselves.

KWL Chart

Directions: Take a minute to think about what you already know about health, hygiene, and nutrition. Write what you know below. Then list some questions you have about this topic that you hope to get answered. After you have finished learning about this topic, you can fill in the last column about what you learned. Perhaps you will get all your questions answered.

What I Know about Health	What I Want to Know about Health	What I've Learned about Health

Name _____ Date _____

My Personal Timeline

Think back to when you were an infant, a toddler, or a preschooler. Do you have memories of losing your first tooth or learning to ride a bike?

Directions: Develop a timeline of your life. Think of physical milestones, such as riding a bike or playing sports; growth areas, such as walking or losing a tooth; or health-related issues, such as sicknesses you have had. Interview family members to help you determine the correct age for each event. Use the timeline below on which to record each event and your age.

My Personal Timeline

_____

_____

0-7424-2757-9 *Health, Hygiene, and Nutrition*

Name _____ Date _____

Sharing My Timeline

Some of your classmates may have had similar life experiences.

Directions: Share your timeline with other students. You will learn a lot about your classmates. Record your findings below.

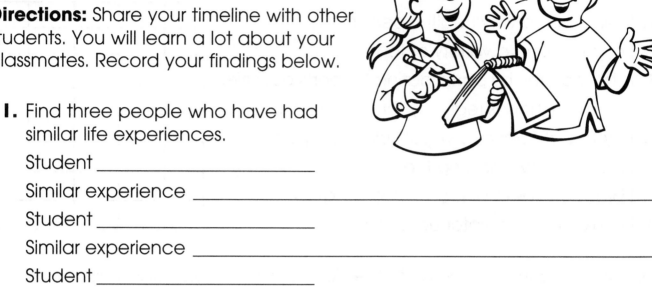

1. Find three people who have had similar life experiences.

   Student _____

   Similar experience _____

   Student _____

   Similar experience _____

   Student _____

   Similar experience _____

2. Find one student about whom you have learned something new from his or her timeline.

   Student _____

   Experience _____

3. Find one student who has done something that you wish you had done.

   Student _____

   Experience _____

4. One of my favorite memories is_____.

Name _____ Date _____

How Healthy Are You?

Directions: Complete the rating scale to assess your overall health.

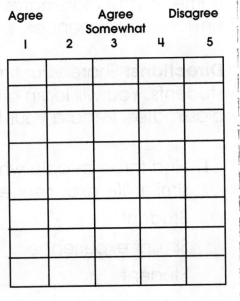

| | Agree | | Agree Somewhat | | Disagree |
	1	2	3	4	5

1. I think I am a very healthy person.

2. I enjoy eating a variety of foods.

3. I stay healthy by participating in sports activities.

4. I wash my hands regularly throughout the day.

5. I try to eat fruits and vegetables every day.

6. I stay safe by following the rules.

7. I brush my teeth at least twice a day.

8. I drink plenty of water each day.

Work with a partner to complete the Venn diagram below. Find out what similiarities and differences you have regarding health, safety, and hygiene.

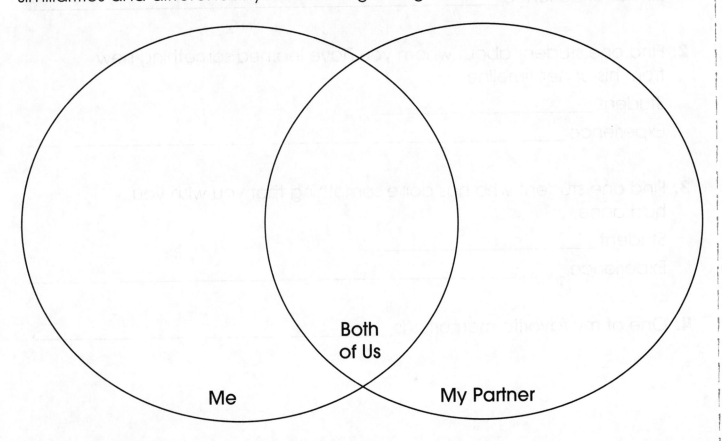

0-7424-2757-9 *Health, Hygiene, and Nutrition*

Name _____ Date _____

Healthy People Scavenger Hunt

Directions: Go on a healthy person scavenger hunt. Talk to students and adults at school or at home about their health. Try to find someone for each category below. Write their names on the lines.

1. I eat broccoli. _____

2. I watch my weight. _____

3. I have recently had a health problem. _____

4. I compete in sports regularly. _____

5. I exercise regularly. _____

6. I have run in a race. _____

7. I believe I am in great shape. _____

8. I used to be a smoker but have quit. _____

9. I take a shower every day. _____

10. I brush my teeth at least twice a day. _____

0-7424-2757-9 *Health, Hygiene, and Nutrition*

Guess Who?

Directions: Answer the questions below about yourself.
Don't let anyone see your answers. Make sure your name is
on the card.

Name_____

If I were a food item, I would be _____.

One of my favorite healthy activities is_____.

Hand in the card after you have filled it
out. Students will read each one aloud
and try to guess who the card is about.

Name _____ Date _____

Your Nutrition

The foods you choose to eat make up your diet. A healthy diet should include a mixture of foods to give your body the right nutrients. Carbohydrates, proteins, and fats help your body grow and give you energy. Vitamins, minerals, and water help your body work properly.

The food pyramid shows the number of daily servings you should eat from each food group. If you follow the food pyramid, your body will get the balanced diet it needs.

Carbohydrates give you energy. There are two kinds of carbohydrates—sugar and starch. Sugars are found in fruit, chocolate, and other sweet foods. Starches are found in bread, rice, pasta, and potatoes. Carbohydrates are broken down into simple sugars. These sugars give your body fuel.

Proteins help your body grow and repair tissues. They are found in meat, eggs, nuts, milk, beans, and fish. When you digest proteins, they are broken down into

smaller acids. These acids are then changed into the energy your body needs to grow.

Fats give your body energy and warmth. The fats that are not used up are stored in your body. There are two kinds of fat—saturated and unsaturated. Saturated fats are found in animal products, such as butter and fatty meat. These also contain cholesterol, which is bad for you. Unsaturated fats are found in nonanimal products, such as vegetable oils and nuts. These are healthy fats.

Food Guide Pyramid

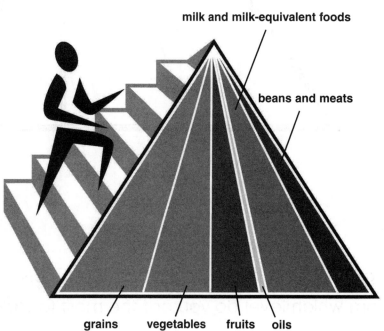

milk and milk-equivalent foods

beans and meats

grains   vegetables   fruits   oils

My Food Pyramid

Directions: Fill in each level of the food pyramid with drawings or pictures of foods cut from magazines.

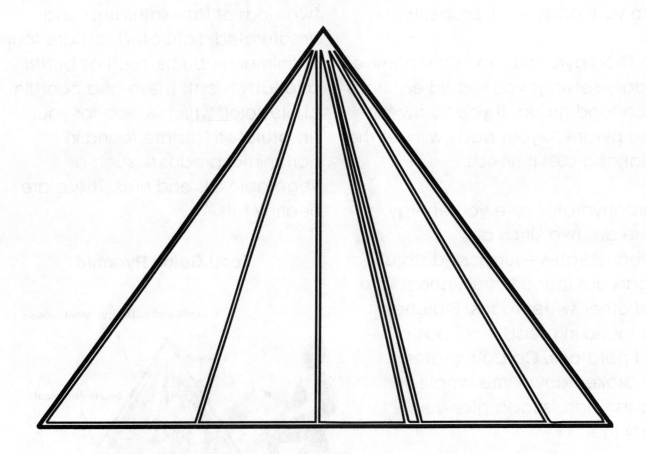

Was one level harder to fill than the others? _____

From which level do you eat the most foods? _____

The Five Food Friends–
Readers' Theater

Narrator 1

Narrator 2

Brianna Bread—My motto: I come from the grain group. I'm an important source of energy. Eat grain!

Michael Meat Eater—My motto: I help you build strong muscles. Eat meat!

Marianne Milky—My motto: I help your body grow strong bones and teeth. Drink milk!

Francis Fruit—My motto: I help your body heal cuts and bruises quickly! Eat fruit!

Veruka Vegetable—My motto: I help your eyes see and your skin stay healthy. Eat vegetables!

Narrator 1: Another day dawns for the Five Food Friends. They are strong and help each other to make children healthy. Today they fly above Central School looking for children who need them. Let's see how they help.

Narrator 2: A student in class didn't eat breakfast. She is sitting with her head down, and she doesn't have enough energy to complete her work. Who can help?

Brianna Bread: I've got my get-up-and-go. I've got my get-up-and-go. It's me! I can help her get the energy she needs to complete her schoolwork!

Narrator 2: So Brianna Bread zooms down to the student with a bowl of healthy grain cereal.

Narrator 1: I see a child whose muscles are sore in dance class. Who can help her?

Michael Meat Eater: My muscles are strong. My muscles are strong. It's me! I can help her grow strong muscles to dance.

Narrator 2: So Michael Meat Eater zooms in to the rescue with some nuts and beans to help her grow strong muscles.

Michael Meat Eater: My job is to help you build strong muscles.

Everyone: **Keeping children healthy!**

Name _____ Date _____

The Five Food Friends–
Readers' Theater (cont.)

Narrator 1: Just then, Marianne Milky spots a young boy walking in from the playground with his arm in a sling.

Marianne Milky: My bones do not break. My bones do not break. They have gotten so strong. Here, son, drink some of this milk. Milk helps you have strong bones and teeth!

Narrator 2: Marianne Milky grins widely as she flies off and calls out . . .

Marianne Milky: Another day of helping kids build strong bones and healthy smiles!

Everyone: **Keeping children healthy!**

Narrator 1: Just then, little Johnny runs to his teacher and says, "Teacher, teacher, I scraped my arm." Francis Fruit wastes no time. She races in with a basket of fruit.

Francis Fruit: Fruit has the power! Fruit has the power! Fruit has the power to heal your cuts! Eating fruit helps to heal your skin! Here, take this orange. Now my job is done.

Everyone: **Keeping children healthy!**

Narrator 2: Now we see that Sarah is having a hard time reading the board in her classroom.

Veruka Vegetable: It's my turn to help! Vegetables help your eyes and skin, eyes and skin, eyes and skin. Vegetables help your eyes and skin, so gobble them up! Look at all your vegetable choices—so many to choose from! Eat your vegetables!

Everyone: **Keeping children healthy!**

Narrator 1: Thus goes another day for the fabulous food group heroes! As they fly into the sunset, they end another day of . . .

Everyone: **Keeping children healthy!**

My Diet

Directions: Use the form below to record everything you eat for three days.

Day 1	Food	Amount	Food Group
Breakfast			
Lunch			
Dinner			

Day 2	Food	Amount	Food Group
Breakfast			
Lunch			
Dinner			

Day 3	Food	Amount	Food Group
Breakfast			
Lunch			
Dinner			

How Much Is an Ounce or a Cup?

Directions: Use the information on ounce and cup serving sizes to calculate whether you ate enough of each food group for the three days you kept track. Write your totals in the table.

Milk, Yogurt, and Cheese

I cup = I cup of milk or yogurt

I cup = 1 1/2 ounces of natural cheese or 2 ounces of processed cheese

Meat, Poultry, Fish, Dry Beans, Eggs, and Nuts

I ounce = I small steak, I small lean hamburger patty, I small chicken breast half

I ounce = 1/4 cup of cooked dry beans

I ounce = I egg

Vegetables

I cup = 2 cups of raw leafy vegetables

I cup = I cup of other vegetables, cooked or raw

I cup = I cup of vegetable juice

Fruits

I cup = I medium apple, banana, or orange

I cup = 32 seedless grapes

I cup = I cup of fruit juice

Bread, Cereal, Rice, and Pasta

I ounce = I slice of bread

I ounce = I cup of ready to eat cereal (flakes or rounds), 1 1/4 cup (puffed)

I ounce = 1/2 cup of cooked cereal, rice, or pasta

Food Groups	Day 1	Day 2	Day 3
Grains			
Fruits			
Vegetables			
Milk			
Meat			
Fats			

How was your diet for the three days? Did you meet the serving recommendations? Do you need to change anything about your diet?

_____

_____

Name _____ Date _____

Nutrition Labels

Directions: Look at this nutrition label for animal crackers. Use the label to answer the following questions.

Nutrition Facts		
Serving Size		10 cookies
Amount Per Serving		
Calories		190
		% Daily Value
Total Fat		7 g
Cholesterol		10 mg
Sodium		130 mg
Total Carbohydrates		31g
Dietary Fiber		0 g
Sugars		19 g
Protein		2 g
Vitamin A 6%	Vitamin C	0%
Calcium 2%	Iron	4%

1. How many animal crackers are equal to one serving? _____

2. How many calories are in one serving? _____

3. Which vitamins and minerals do animal crackers provide? _____

4. How much cholesterol is in a serving of animal crackers? _____

5. If you ate two servings of this food, how many crackers would you eat?

_____

If you ate four servings, how many crackers is that? _____

6. What other information did you notice on the food label? _____

_____

How else is the label helpful?

_____

_____

_____

0-7424-2757-9 *Health, Hygiene, and Nutrition*

Facts from the Bread Group

The foods from the bread group give you energy for learning and playing. Foods in this group are made from different grains, such as wheat, oats, rye, barley, and rice. These foods have complex carbohydrates, which are an important source of energy, especially in low-fat diets. These foods also have vitamins, minerals, and fiber. The food guide pyramid suggests 4-6 ounces a day. Take a look at what kinds of foods you eat from this group. Be careful—some foods from this group, such as croissants and muffins, do not provide the best nutrition. They are also very high in fat.

Sugar versus Starch

When you eat foods that are high in sugar, the food is absorbed
into your body quickly, but then you feel hungry again quickly.

Directions: Fill two glasses halfway with cornstarch. Add red food coloring to both glasses. This represents the blood in your body. Add one teaspoon of flour to one glass. Add one teaspoon of sugar to the other glass. Record your observations in the space below.

_____   _____

_____   _____

_____   _____

A Breakfast to See Me Through the Morning

Do you want to find out which foods you can eat for breakfast that will keep you energized until lunch?

Directions: Conduct an experiment with your breakfast over a two-week period. Eat sweet foods, such as dougnuts or sugary cereal, on some days. Eat healthy foods, such as whole grain bread or cereal, on other days. Experiment by adding fruit, juice, or milk to see if that has an effect on you. Record the time you ate, the food you ate, and the time you were hungry again. Before you begin, make a prediction below.

I predict that a breakfast of _____
will keep me energized until lunchtime.

Day	Food	Sugary or Healthy	Time I Ate	Time I Got Hungry
1				
2				
3				
4				
5				
6				
7				
8				
9				
10				
11				
12				
13				
14				

Was your prediction correct? _____

What did you learn? _____

Cereal Choices

Directions: Bring in the nutritional information for your favorite cereal. As a class, compare the cereals and fill in the chart below. Write the cereal name at the top of a column. Write the percentage of each vitamin and mineral in the cereals you've chosen. Do this for three different cereals.

Vitamin A			
Vitamin C			
Calcium			
Iron			
Vitamin D			
Thiamin			
Riboflavin			
Niacin			
Vitamin B_6			
Folic Acid			
Phosphorus			
Magnesium			
Zinc			
Copper			

Which cereal is the healthiest? _____

the least healthiest? _____

Name _____ Date _____

Starch Test

Materials Needed:
cornstarch, potatoes, bread, crackers, cheese,
cooked egg white, paper plates

Starches are the only digestible complex carbohydrate
found in foods. When they are present in foods, they give
your body the vitamins and minerals that you need.

Directions: Test some foods to see if they contain starch.
Look at the foods in front of you. Draw a picture of some
of the foods. Label each food.

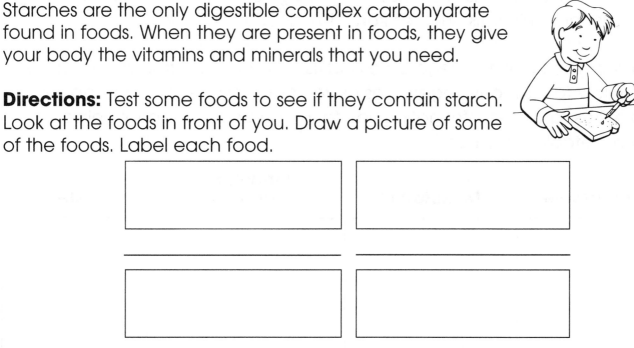

Working in a group, put a drop of tincture of iodine on each
food item. Observe what happens. Draw your observations below.
Write a short description of what you see.

Did any of the foods turn black or blue black? If so, these
foods contain starch.

0-7424-2757-9 *Health, Hygiene, and Nutrition*

Facts from the Vegetable Group

Vegetables keep your eyes healthy and give you healthy skin. Vegetables can be found as leaves, stalks, roots, flowers, and seeds. They provide vitamins, such as vitamins A and folate, and minerals, such as iron and magnesium. They are naturally low in fat and contain fiber. Eating vegetables may help protect you from heart disease and cancer. The food guide pyramid suggests eating $1\frac{1}{2}$ - $2\frac{1}{2}$ cups a day.

Directions: Look at each vegetable and its nutritional information. Fill in the chart below for as many vegetables as you can. Taste each vegetable if possible. Based on the information you found and your personal opinion, which vegetable is the best?

Vegetable	Description	Nutritional Information	Taste

Cooked versus Raw

> **Materials Needed:**
> various vegetables, cooked and raw
> samples of each one

If you were offered cooked vegetables or raw vegetables, which would you choose? How does cooking vegetables change the way they look? Is one way of eating them more nutritious for you?

Directions: Look at each vegetable in its raw state and cooked state. Does a vegetable look different after it has been cooked? Does it taste differently? Fill in the chart below about each vegetable.

Vegetable	Look	Taste
raw carrots		
cooked carrots		

Raw vegetables are better for you than cooked vegetables.
Why? _____

Facts from the Fruit Group

Foods from the fruit group help your body heal cuts and bruises. Your skin protects your body from germs, so you need to keep your skin healthy. Fruit and fruit juices provide important amounts of vitamins A and C, potassium, and fiber. Fruit and fruit juices are low in fat and contain little sodium (salt). The food guide pyramid suggests eating 1 - 1½ cups a day.

Directions: Conduct a blind taste test of juice. In your group, take turns tasting the juice samples. Rate them in order of best-tasting to worst-tasting. Write your first and second choices in the chart below. Do this for each member of your group. As a group, reveal which juice is which. Look at the nutritional information for each sample. Did everyone like the 100 percent juice better than the other juices?

Group Member	1st Choice	2nd Choice

Answer the following questions.

1. What can you conclude about the different juices? _____

2. Do any of the results surprise you? _____

Name _____ Date _____

Fruit Juice Fun

Directions: Make your own orange juice using different percentages of juice and water. Mix the orange juice with water according to the percentages below. Taste each one. Write a description of how it looks and tastes. Then answer the questions.

10% juice	1 tbsp orange juice	9 tbsp water
25% juice	1 tbsp orange juice	3 tbsp water
50% juice	1 tbsp orange juice	1 tbsp water
100% juice	all orange juice	no water

10% juice
looks _____

tastes _____

25% juice
looks _____

tastes _____

50% juice
looks _____

tastes _____

100% juice
looks _____

tastes _____

Answer the following questions.

1. Which juice did you like best? Why? _____

2. How did the juices change with less water? _____

3. In juices that are less than 100 percent juice, what other ingredient might be in them? _____

Published by Instructional Fair. Copyright protected.   0-7424-2757-9 *Health, Hygiene, and Nutrition*

Name _____ Date _____

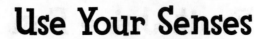

Use Your Senses

Directions: Use all five senses to write a descriptive paragraph about a vegetable or fruit of your choice. Before writing, fill in the web below about the vegetable or fruit. Write the food you have chosen in the middle circle. Write descriptive words in the outer circles about how the food looks, smells, feels, and tastes. Include this information, as well as why you chose this food, in your paragraph below the web.

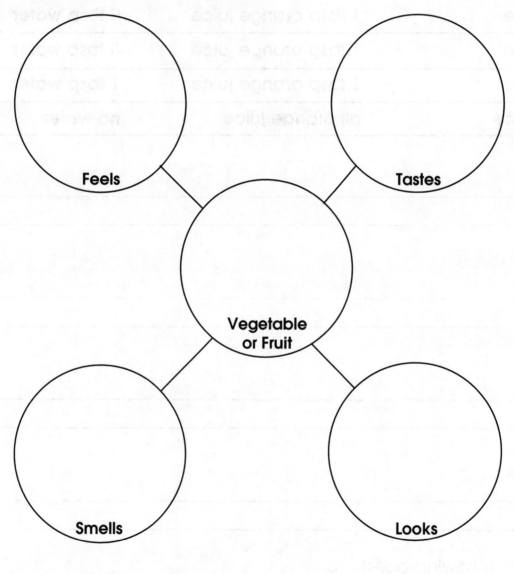

Feels

Tastes

Vegetable or Fruit

Smells

Looks

_____

_____

_____

_____

0-7424-2757-9 *Health, Hygiene, and Nutrition*

Facts from the Dairy Group

The dairy group helps your body produce strong bones and teeth. Dairy products provide your body with protein, vitamins, and minerals. One of the most important minerals your body needs is found in dairy products. This mineral is calcium. Calcium is what makes your bones strong and healthy. The food group pyramid suggests eating 2–3 cups of dairy a day. Milk, yogurt, and cheese are the best sources of calcium.

Directions: Create a poster to convince people to eat dairy products every day. Use the information above. Make your poster look delicious.

Name _____ Date _____

Checking Out Calcium

Materials Needed:
samples of limestone, chalk, and marble;
magnifying glasses

Calcium is a mineral that makes your bones and teeth strong. It is found in the foods from the dairy group, such as yogurt, cheese, and milk.

Directions: Some rocks contain calcium. Do an experiment to find out which of the rocks in front of you contain calcium. In a group, follow the steps below.

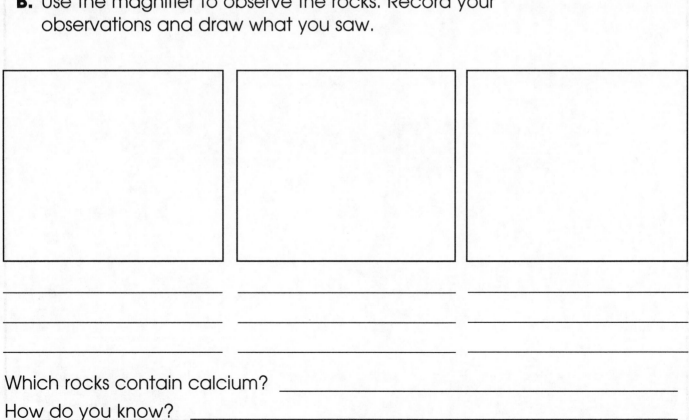

A. Place two drops of vinegar on each sample of limestone, chalk, and marble.

B. Use the magnifier to observe the rocks. Record your observations and draw what you saw.

_____ _____ _____

_____ _____ _____

_____ _____ _____

Which rocks contain calcium? _____

How do you know? _____

Published by Instructional Fair. Copyright protected.   0-7424-2757-9 *Health, Hygiene, and Nutrition*

Name _____ Date _____

Milk Confusion

Not all milk is created equal. Some milk is thinner than other milk. Some milk contains more fat than others. So why would you choose one over the other?

Directions: Look at the nutrition labels of the three different types of milk in front of you—whole milk, 2%, and ¹/₂% milk.

Whole Milk	2% Reduced-Fat Milk	1/2% Milk
Nutrition Facts	**Nutrition Facts**	**Nutrition Facts**
Serving Size I cup	Serving Size I cup	Serving Size I cup
Calories 150	Calories 130	Calories 100
Total Fat 8g	Total Fat 5g	Total Fat 1g
Cholesterol 35mg	Cholesterol 20mg	Cholesterol 10mg
Sodium 125mg	Sodium 125mg	Sodium 130mg
Total Carbohydrates 13g	Total Carbohydrates 13g	Total Carbohydrates 13g
Dietary Fiber 0g	Dietary Fiber 0g	Dietary Fiber 0g
Sugars 12g	Sugars 12g	Sugars 12g
Protein 8g	Protein 8g	Protein 9g

Answer the following questions.

1. What are some differences you notice by looking at the labels?

_____

2. Which milk would you chose based on the labels?

_____

3. Which milk do you think is the healthiest? Why? _____

_____

Published by Instructional Fair. Copyright protected.   0-7424-2757-9 *Health, Hygiene, and Nutrition*

Name _____ Date _____

Facts from the Protein Group

Materials Needed:
one walnut, cashew, and pecan for each group
of students; one metal bowl per group, three corks
per group; needles; matches; thermometers

Foods from the protein group help you build strong muscles. Meat, poultry, and fish supply your body with protein, B vitamins, iron, and zinc. The other foods in this group, such as dry beans, eggs, and nuts, also provide you with protein and most vitamins and minerals. You have about 650 muscles in your body. Muscles hold your bones together and make them move. It is important to keep your muscles strong and healthy. The food guide pyramid suggests eating 3-5 ounces of protein a day.

Directions: Nuts contain a great deal of energy in the form of oils. When you eat nuts, your body uses this energy. To determine which of these three nuts—a walnut, pecan, or cashew—gives off the most energy, conduct the following experiment.

A. Stick a needle in the end of each nut. Stick the other end of the needle into a piece of cork.

B. Put ¹/₄ of an inch of water in the bottom of a small metal bowl.

C. Measure the temperature of the water in the bowl with a thermometer. Write the temperature below.

D. Under adult supervision, light one of the nuts with a match. Carefully hold the bowl over the flame. Use tongs if the metal gets too hot.

E. When the nut stops burning, take the temperature of the water again. Record the temperature below.

F. Compare the starting water temperature to the ending water temperature. Write the difference below.

G. Let the water and bowl cool down. Repeat the steps for the other nuts.

Starting water temperature: _____
Record the temperature for each nut:

Walnut _____ Pecan _____ Cashew _____
Difference of _____ Difference of _____ Difference of _____

Digestive Discoveries

Materials Needed:
a small piece of cooked lean beef for each
student, bottles with screw caps, dark cola

Your digestive system works to break
down foods you eat. While you chew
and swallow foods, different acids in
your saliva and stomach work to break
down the foods.

Directions: Acids bread down protein
that is found in meat. Follow the steps
below to observe how the meat you eat
is digested (broken down).

A. Place a small piece of cooked lean
   beef in a bottle.

B. Pour cola into the bottle.

C. Screw on the lid to seal the cola
   and meat.

D. Observe the cola and meat for one week. Do not open
   the bottle during this time. Record your observations below.

Discuss the following questions.
1. Do you think that meat is easy to digest?

2. What other foods might be easier for your body to digest?

3. With what other foods could you do this experiment?

Name _____   Date _____

Breaking Down Digestion

The digestive system is made up of many parts that work together. The teeth, esophagus, stomach, small intestine, pancreas, large intestine, and colon all have their own roles in digestion. Do you know what each one does?

Directions: Choose one of the digestive system parts to research. Use an encyclopedia, the Internet, or the library to find information for your research. Use the web below on which to organize your information. Then write your report on another piece of paper.

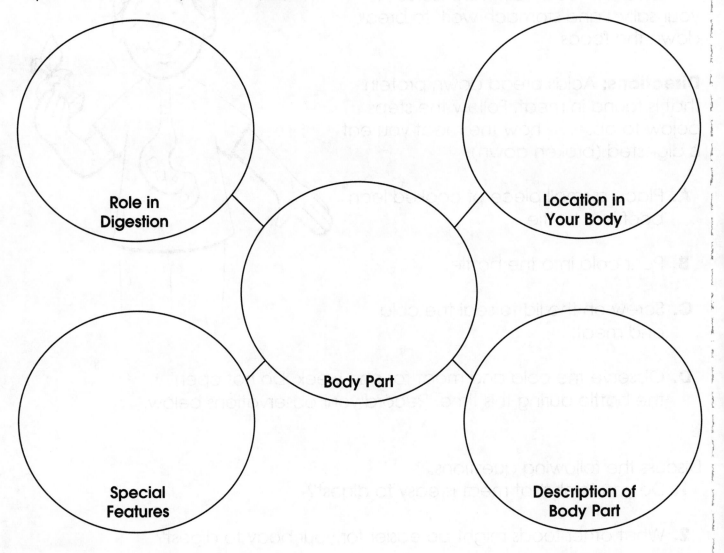

Facts from the Fat Group

Materials Needed:
margarine, lettuce, bacon, nuts,
crackers, brown paper bags

Even though this food group is given the smallest
amount of room on the food pyramid, it is
probably the most popular. The fat group
includes foods such as potato chips, cookies,
candy, pop, chocolate, and other junk food.
These foods don't help you build muscles or
protect your body from illness, but they are a
nice treat once in a while. You are supposed to
eat sparingly from this group, which means you
should eat only a little. Too much of a good
thing from this group can be bad.

Directions: To find out if foods have oil or fat in
them, do the following experiment.
  A. Feel each food in front of you, one at a time.
  B. After feeling each food, rub your fingers together. If your
    fingers are oily or slippery, that food contains fat.
  C. Next, rub each piece of food on a piece of brown paper bag.
  D. Hold the bag up to the light. Is it transparent (clear) where
    you rubbed the food? If it is, that food contains fat.

Answer the following questions.
  1. Which of these foods do you think contains the most fat? _____
    the least fat? _____
  2. What other foods could you use in this experiment to show that they
    contain fat? _____
  3. What are a few of your favorite foods from the fat food group?

  _____

French Fry Fat Test

Materials Needed:
French fry samples (fast-food and frozen)

How do French fries from different restaurants measure up? Are they all the same? Are baked French fries any different from restaurant French fries? Let's do an experiment to find out.

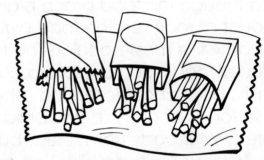

Directions: Create your own fat test. Develop a way to measure the amount of fat in different French fry samples. List the steps below to show how you will go about measuring the fat in the samples. Add more steps if needed. Then conduct your experiment.

A.

B.

C.

D.

E.

Answer the following questions.

1. Was your experiment successful? _____

2. What did your experiment show you? _____

3. How would you change your experiment if you did it again? _____

Sweet as Can Be

Materials Needed:
apple juice, corn syrup, chopped onion, crackers,
test tubes, candles, matches, Benedict's solution
(available at science supply stores)

Directions: To find out which foods below contain simple sugars, follow these steps.

A. Place a small amount of each of these foods in separate test tubes: apple juice, corn syrup, cracker, onion.
B. Add five drops of Benedict's solution to each test tube.
C. Have an adult help you heat the test tube over a candle.
D. Observe what happens.
E. Record your findings below.

Apple juice _____

_____

Corn syrup _____

_____

Cracker _____

_____

Onion _____

_____

Did any of the foods turn yellow or brick red after you added the Benedict's solution? If so, these contain simple sugars.

0-7424-2757-9 *Health, Hygiene, and Nutrition*

Name _____ Date _____

Sugar by Any Other Name

In foods that contain sugar, the sugar can be called many different things on the nutrition label. It can be called corn syrup, maltose, sucrose, fructose, corn sweetener, syrup, dextrose, glucose, lactose, or molasses. The information on a food label is also listed in a certain order—from the most abundant to the least abundant ingredient.

Directions: Look at the foods in the chart. Predict how much sugar you think each one has. Place a check mark in the box to show your prediction—I being no sugar at all, 3 being somewhat sugary, and 5 being loaded with sugar. Then check the nutrition labels for each food. Were your predictions correct?

Food	I	2	3	4	5
candy bar					
soda					
fruit punch					
popcorn					
peanut butter					
yogurt					

Aim to eat 10–40 grams of sugar a day. If you go over 40 grams of sugar, you've eaten too much.

0-7424-2757-9 Health, Hygiene, and Nutrition

Regular versus Low-Fat

A calorie is the unit of energy that a food contains. All nutrition labels show how many calories a food has. Most nutrition labels also show the percentage of the food's total calories that come from fat.

Directions: Gather nutrition labels from five different foods, such as chips, crackers, cheese, soup, salad dressing, and candy. For each food item, find a low-fat version. Collect these labels as well. Use the chart to record the calories from fat for both the regular and low-fat foods.

Food	Regular	Low-Fat

Answer the following questions.

1. Which foods have less calories from fat—regular or low-fat? _____

2. Which foods in your chart contain the most calories from fat?

_____

3. Would you consider switching to the low-fat version of each food in your chart? Why or why not? _____

Name _____ Date _____

Roll for Your Food

Your diet is not something you should leave to chance. Your health and well-being are too important to do that.

Directions: Play this game to see what can happen if you gamble with your diet.

Game Rules

A. Roll one die.
B. Match the number you rolled to the food group in the food pyramid.
C. Choose a food from this group that you would eat.
D. Write it in the chart below.
E. Roll again and repeat the steps.
F. After 21 rolls, look at your diet for the day.
G. Answer the questions below.

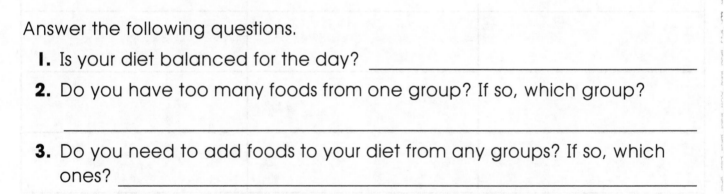

Answer the following questions.

1. Is your diet balanced for the day? _____

2. Do you have too many foods from one group? If so, which group?

_____

3. Do you need to add foods to your diet from any groups? If so, which ones? _____

4. What does this game show you about choosing what you eat?

_____

Grains	Fruit	Vegetable	Dairy	Protein	Fats

Published by Instructional Fair. Copyright protected.
0-7424-2757-9 Health, Hygiene, and Nutrition

Name _____ Date _____

The Best Selection

You have a lot of choices about the foods you eat. Each food group offers unlimited choices. A slice of wheat bread and a piece of coffee cake are both from the grain group. Is one healthier than the other? Look at the labels below to see how the two foods compare.

Whole Wheat Bread Nutrition Facts	
Serving Size	1 slice
Calories	80
Total Fat	1g
Cholesterol	0mg
Sodium	160mg
Total Carbohydrates	15g
Dietary Fiber	1g
Sugars	2g
Protein	3g

Coffee Cake Nutrition Facts	
Serving Size	1 piece
Calories	200
Total Fat	9g
Cholesterol	35mg
Sodium	190mg
Total Carbohydrates	25g
Dietary Fiber	less than 1g
Sugars	12g
Protein	4g

Directions: Answer the questions about the food labels.

1. Which food appears to be a healthier choice? _____

Why? _____

2. What are some benefits of the wheat bread? _____

3. What are some benefits of the coffee cake? _____

4. What is one noticeable difference between the two foods that you see on the labels? _____

Choose two other foods from a different food group to compare, such as yogurt and cheese or chicken and steak. Write a short summary of how the two foods compare. _____

_____

_____

_____

Published by Instructional Fair. Copyright protected.

0-7424-2757-9 *Health, Hygiene, and Nutrition*

Healthy Creation Contest

Many snack foods, such as chips and cookies, are not healthy. What do you like to snack on that is healthy?

Directions: As a group, create a new, unique healthy snack. Agree on a snack name. List the ingredients below. List the steps, in order, that it takes to create the snack. Then create a poster to promote your new snack. Lure people to want to try it.

Snack name: _____

Ingredients:

Snack-Making Steps

A. _____

B. _____

C. _____

D. _____

E. _____

Fast-Food Frenzy

Directions: Pick a meal (with side dishes) from a fast-food restaurant. Look at the nutrition facts for the meal. This can be obtained at the restaurant or on the Internet. List the information for the foods in the chart below.

Food	Vitamins/Minerals	Calories	Fat

Directions: Answer the questions about the meal you chose.

1. Is this a healthy meal? Why or why not?_____

_____

2. How could it be healthier? _____

_____

Now choose another meal from the same restaurant. Fill in the chart below and compare the two meals. Then answer the questions.

Food	Vitamins/Minerals	Calories	Fat

3. Which meal is healthier? _____

4. What makes this meal healthier? _____

5. Which meal would you choose in the future? Why? _____

Name _____ Date _____

Create Your Own Restaurant

Directions: Create a restaurant, complete with your very own menu. Give your diners meal choices (entrée and a side dish). Make the meals healthy—try to follow the food pyramid when creating each meal. Write the menu in the space below.

Name _____ Date _____

Favorite Foods Data

What is your favorite food? Do you think other students in your class have the same favorite food as you?

Directions: Take a survey of the students in your classroom to determine everyone's favorite foods. It might be an entrée, such as a hamburger, or it might be a snack or dessert, such as popcorn or cake. Keep track of everyone's answers in the chart below. Then create a graph on a separate sheet of paper that shows your results. Make sure you give your graph a title and label both axes.

Student	Favorite Food

0-7424-2757-9 *Health, Hygiene, and Nutrition*

Name _____ Date _____

Healthy America?

You live in a society where anything you want is within reach—including food. This may be one reason why so many Americans are considered obese.

Directions: Examine the eating habits of your family members and friends. Create a survey to learn about their eating habits. Address the following questions in your survey. Then write your survey below.

- How frequently do you eat fast food?
- How frequently do you eat frozen dinners?
- How often do you eat snack foods?
- How many fruits and vegetables do you eat each day?

Name	Fast Food	Frozen Dinner	Snack Foods	Fruits and Vegetables

0-7424-2757-9 *Health, Hygiene, and Nutrition*

Nutrition Review

Directions: Answer the questions about nutrition.

1. Proteins help your body grow and repair tissue. Proteins are found in
   a. meat.
   b. nuts.
   c. beans.
   d. all of the above.

2. The food pyramid has _____ sections. (circle one)   3   4   6

3. The fats food group provides your body with
   a. energy for growing strong bodies.
   b. calcium for growing strong bones.
   c. little or no nutrients to make your body strong and healthy.

4. From which food group do you need the most servings in one day?
   a. protein group
   b. grain group
   c. dairy group

5. Match the food group to the health benefits it provides.

   Dairy Group   These foods help my body heal cuts and bruises.

   Protein Group   These foods help me to have good eyesight.

   Vegetable Group   These foods give me energy.

   Fruit Group   These foods help build strong muscles.

   Grain Group   These foods help me grow strong bones and teeth.

6. Write a summary of why it is important to follow the food pyramid.

   _____

   _____

   _____

   _____

Your Health

Your body is made up of a number of systems that work together. Each system performs a different job to keep you healthy.

The respiratory system is made up of your lungs and the passages that lead to them. When you breathe in, you inhale air through your nose and mouth down a tube called the windpipe, or trachea. The air goes into your lungs. Oxygen from the air passes into your blood. Your blood then carries oxygen through your body. When you breathe out, you exhale carbon dioxide from your body.

Your circulatory system is made up of blood, blood vessels, and the heart. This system moves oxygen-rich blood through your body. Your blood travels through tubes called blood vessels. Your heart, which is a muscular organ, pumps blood to all parts of your body. The heart is divided into four spaces, called chambers. The two upper chambers are called the atria. The two lower chambers are called the ventricles.

Muscles are the stretchy tissue that is found throughout your body. They are responsible for making your body move. Some muscles are voluntary, such as the muscles to lift your leg. Other muscles, such as your heart, are involuntary muscles. These work automatically. Your body contains about 640 muscles that are attached to the skeleton of your body. These help your body move.

The digestive system breaks down food to supply your body with the energy and nutrients it needs for growth and repair. After your teeth break food through smaller pieces, your tongue collects the food into a ball that you swallow. The food moves down the throat, through the esophagus, and into the stomach. The stomach, which can hold 2 to 4 liters of food, kneads the food and adds liquid to make it soupy. The food then passes into a narrow tube called the small intestine. This is the longest part of the digestive system. The food is broken down into particles small enough to be absorbed into the bloodstream.

Germaine's Travels

Before reading the following story aloud, talk about germs. Where do they live? How do they get around? What can they do to people? Get a feeling for how much your students know about germs. After the story, discuss how a germ travels and how students can protect themselves from germs.

Once upon a time, there lived a germ on a grocery store cart. His name was Germaine. Germaine was never lonely. He was always surrounded by millions of his friends. His friends lived on tables, chairs, food, and people. They lived on anything they could cling to.

But Germaine was ready for a change of scenery. "Here's my ride," he called, as a boy walked toward the cart. He clung to the boy's hand when he grabbed the cart handle. But the boy's mom told him it was time to go to the bathroom and wash his hands. Germaine jumped onto the handle of the bathroom door.

Germaine's journey continued when a young girl grabbed the door handle by accident. "Here I go," yelled Germaine. As the girl reached up to scratch her nose, Germaine yelled, "Jackpot! Now is my chance to get inside her and make her sick."

Just then, the girl sneezed: "AaaAaaAaaChoo! " Germaine was rocketed across the room onto an apple. "What a ride," he said.

As he was catching his breath, a giant mouth opened up over him. He was being gobbled up. Germaine made his way through the person's body, excited to finally make someone sick.

Suddenly, out of nowhere, Germaine was being followed. "Oh, no—white blood cells! I'm finished now." That was the end of Germaine's journey.

Name _____ Date _____

Your Body's Defenses

Germs are very small organisms that you cannot see with the naked eye. In order to see them, you need to use a very powerful microscope.

Germs can make you sick, but your body has special defenses to help prevent you from getting sick. These defenses are your skin, nose, mouth and throat, and special cells in your body.

Your skin is a natural barrier against germs. The only time your skin doesn't protect you from germs is when you have a cut. Germs can enter your body through a cut.

Your nose helps protect you from germs because it is lined with tiny hairs. When you breathe in through your nose, germs get caught in the hairs.

Your mouth and throat also help keep you healthy. They are wet and sticky. Germs get stuck in your throat and mouth and can't travel any further into your body.

When germs do make it into your body, two types of cells in your blood fight the germs. White blood cells attack harmful germs. Antibodies attack germs with which they have come in contact before. For example, if you have already had the chicken pox, your body has created antibodies that will attack those germs so they do not make you sick again.

Directions: Write a summary of how different parts of your body protect you from germs. _____

_____

_____

0-7424-2757-9 *Health, Hygiene, and Nutrition*

Name _____ Date _____

They're in Your Blood

Your body holds about 4 to 5 liters of blood. That's more than two 2-liter bottles of soda. Inside your blood, cells and platelets are floating around. There are white and red blood cells. The white blood cells, which are larger than red blood cells, fight disease and help to protect you when you get sick. Red blood cells are disk-shaped cells that contain hemoglobin. These cells carry oxygen through your body. Platelets are tiny fragments of cells. They help stop the bleeding when you cut yourself.

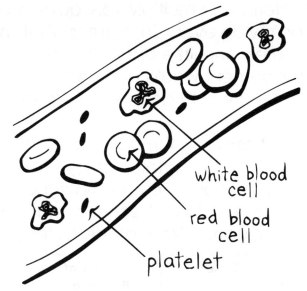

white blood cell

red blood cell

platelet

Directions: Fill in the blanks and answer the questions.

1. _____ blood cells carry oxygen through your body.

2. If you cut yourself, _____ help stop the bleeding.

3. Chicken pox can be fought off by _____ blood cells if you have had the illness before.

4. How much blood does your body hold? _____

5. What could happen if your body was low on white blood cells?

   _____

   _____

6. What could happen if your blood did not contain any platelets?

   _____

   _____

Name _____ Date _____

Germs Multiply

Bacteria can multiply very quickly. Under the best conditions, they can divide every 20 minutes. That means that after just 20 minutes, one little bacteria that was growing in a good growth environment would double to two. After 20 more minutes, the two bacteria would double to four. This can continue indefinitely.

Directions: Use the ball of clay in front of you to represent one bacterium. Divide it in half after holding it for 30 seconds. In the chart below, record how many bacteria you have now. Wait another 30 seconds. Divide each of those bacteria. Record how many bacteria you have now after a total of 60 seconds. Repeat these steps to fill in the chart.

Time	Number of Bacteria
30 sec.	2
1 min.	
1 1/2 min.	
2 min.	
2 1/2 min.	
3 min.	
3 1/2 min.	
4 min.	
4 1/2 min.	
5 min.	

Time	Number of Bacteria
5 1/2	
6 min.	
6 1/2 min.	
7 min.	
7 1/2 min.	
8 min.	
8 1/2 min.	
9 min.	
9 1/2 min.	
10 min.	

Answer the following questions.

1. How do you think you could control the growth of bacteria?

_____

_____

2. How many bacteria could grow in five minutes? _____
ten minutes? _____

0-7424-2757-9 *Health, Hygiene, and Nutrition*

Name _____ Date _____

Catch a Germ

Germs are everywhere. Even though you can't see them, germs are on doorknobs, pencils, shoes, books, balls, and even your hands. Follow the directions for Glitter Ball to see just how easy it is for germs to be on everything.

Directions for Glitter Ball
  A. Choose a partner.
  B. Cover a ball with petroleum jelly and glitter.
  C. Throw the ball back and forth for a few minutes.
  D. Walk around the room and touch things, such as a doorknob, an eraser, desks, windows, and a faucet.
  E. Answer the questions below.

Answer the following questions.
  1. What did this experiment show you? _____
  _____

  2. What did you notice about everything you touched? _____
  _____

  3. What did you learn about keeping yourself clean and healthy?
  _____

  4. Explain how germs are transferred from one object to another.
  _____
  _____

 0-7424-2757-9 *Health, Hygiene, and Nutrition*

Name _____ Date _____

Hand-Washing Habits

Hand washing is one of the best ways to stop the spread of germs. It is the best defense against infections that are spread by hand-to-hand contact. A survey conducted by the American Society of Microbiology found that up to 30 percent of people do not wash their hands in airports across the United States. But a different phone survey reported that 95 percent of people said they washed their hands in public restrooms.

What do you consider to be a good hand washing? It is recommended that you wash your hands for 10 to 15 seconds. (The soap plus the scrubbing jiggles the germs free.) Then dry your hands well.

Directions: Create a poster and a slogan for hand washing. Promote how to do hand washing correctly and why it is important.

0-7424-2757-9 *Health, Hygiene, and Nutrition*

Name _____ Date _____

Rate the Hand Washing

How do you know if your hands are dirty? Sometimes you can see the dirt, but other times you can't see what is on your hands.

Directions: In your group, rate how clean each other's hands are. Create a chart and rating scale below to show your results.

Have one student in your group be the volunteer hand washer. He will spread one teaspoon of washable paint on his hands, including the front and back, and in between his fingers. After the paint has dried, blindfold the hand washer. Then follow the steps below.

A. Have him wash his hands in warm water for one second. Blot dry.
B. Other group members observe and rate his hands using the rating scale.
C. Have the hand washer wash his hands in water for four more seconds. Blot dry.
D. Other group members observe and rate his hands again.
E. Have the hand washer wash his hands in water for 15 seconds. Blot dry.
F. Other group members observe and rate his hands again.
G. Have the hand washer repeat the experiment using soap and water.

Answer the following questions.

1. What did you observe happening as the hand washer washed his hands without soap? _____

2. What happened when the hand washer used soap? _____

_____

3. What is the importance of using soap when washing your hands?

_____

_____

School Illnesses

Directions: What illnesses have you had during the last two years? List them below and write about the steps you took to get better.

1. Illness _____

_____

2. Illness _____

_____

3. Illness _____

_____

4. Illness _____

_____

Research a common illness. Use an encyclopedia or the Internet to find information. Write your information below.

Illness name: _____

_____

Common causes: _____

_____

Bacteria/Viral: _____

Symptoms:_____

_____

Recommended treatments: _____

_____

_____

Hand-Washing Comic Strip

Directions: Your little sister does not know how to wash her hands correctly. Using what you know about hand washing, create a comic strip below that shows exactly how your sister should do it. For each picture, write a sentence describing what she should do.

55

0-7424-2757-9 *Health, Hygiene, and Nutrition*

Cold Control

Everyone comes in contact with germs every day. To demonstrate this fact, do the following activity with your students.

Select three students in your class and pull them aside. Tell them that they have a bad cold, but they are not to reveal this to their classmates. The rest of the class should be unaware of this.

Then select two students to be the Cold Control. For a designated amount of time, these students will observe the sick students going about their daily business.

While the Cold Control students are observing, they should keep track of each person the sick people touch, as well as whom those people touch. They can create a graph in which to record this information.

Eventually, reveal to your students the experiment they have done. Have the Cold Control reveal who was touched and by whom. As a class, brainstorm a list of things sick people can do to help keep others healthy, as well as things healthy people can do around sick people to protect themselves from getting sick.

Name _____ Date _____

Let's Grow Bacteria

Directions: What are the conditions needed for bacteria to grow? Grow mold and compare it with the growth of germs. Follow the steps below.

A. Place three slices of bread in three sandwich bags. Label the bags A, B, and C.
B. Place Bag A in a dark place.
C. Place Bag B in the refrigerator.
D. Put a few drops of water on the bread in Bag C and place it in a dark place.
E. Observe the bags for four days. Write your observations below.

Observations	Bag A	Bag B	Bag C
Day 1			
Day 2			
Day 3			
Day 4			

Answer the following questions.

1. Which piece of bread grew the most mold?_____

2. Why do you think it grew the most mold? _____

3. Where should you store bread to keep it fresh? _____

4. What conditions are favorable for mold growth?_____

0-7424-2757-9 *Health, Hygiene, and Nutrition*

The Big Sneeze

Read this poem aloud about Ronald, the big sneezer. Then talk about how germs are spread through sneezes.

Ronald was not feeling well today.
His nose was runny, his sneezes would spray!
He sneezed by the sink and the fountain, too.
At lunch, he sneezed on me and on you!
Finally, we cried, "Don't spray your germs on us!
They'll make us sick. Then we surely will fuss."

To demonstrate the spray of a sneeze, squirt water from a spray bottle into the air while your students watch. For each squirt described below, make observations as a class about how far the water sprayed and what objects got wet. Make a chart on the board similar to the one below and record some observations. Then make a list of recommendations on how students can best protect others around them from germs when they sneeze.

Spray Bottle Facing Down	Spray Bottle Facing Up	Partially Covered Spray Bottle

0-7424-2757-9 *Health, Hygiene, and Nutrition*

A Germ Story

Directions: Create a story about a germ. Will it be funny? Will it be scary? Will it be mysterious? To help prepare for writing, fill in the story web below with your ideas. Fill in the outer sections with one word or phrase per section. Then use this information to write your story on another piece of paper. Write your title in the middle of the web.

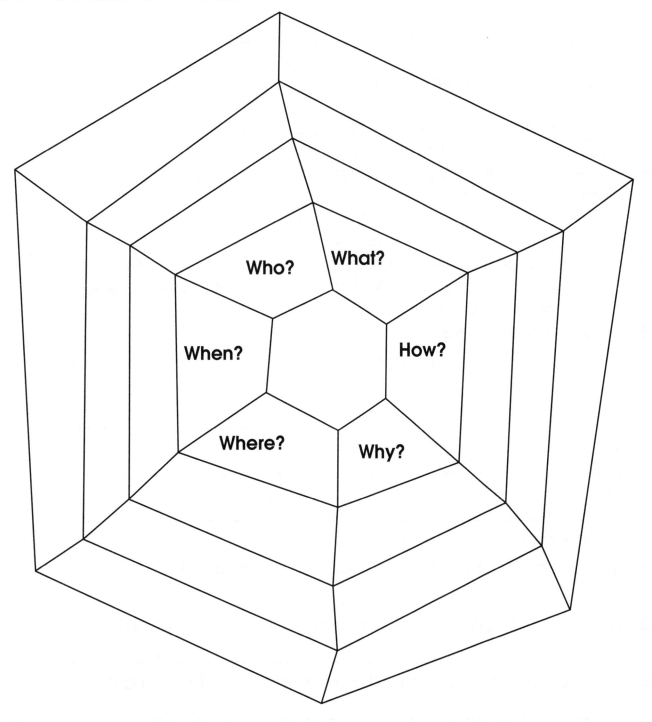

59

0-7424-2757-9 *Health, Hygiene, and Nutrition*

An A-Peeling Skin

Name _____ Date _____

Your skin is the largest organ in your body. It covers your body and protects it from being damaged, getting infected, and drying out. It also prevents germs from entering your body. But germs can enter your body through a cut or a scrape. This is why it is important to keep your skin clean and healthy.

Directions: The skin on an apple protects the apple in much the same way your skin protects your body. Perform the following experiment to see how important your skin is to your health.

A. In a small group, get two apples. Scrape the skin of both apples with a fork. Cut a hole in each apple.

B. Place one apple in a plastic bag and seal it. Label this the Healthy Apple.

C. Pass the second apple around to all of the group members. Group members should rub the apple on items they think have germs.

D. Seal the second apple in a bag and label it the Germ Apple.

E. Observe the two apples over a three-day period. Record your observations in the chart below.

F. Answer the questions.

Day	Healthy Apple	Germ Apple
1		
2		
3		

Answer the following questions.

1. How does your skin help to protect you from germs?

_____

2. Why is it important to keep your skin healthy and cut-free?

_____

3. How can you protect yourself from germs if you have a cut?

_____

Skin Cells

Your skin has two main layers—the outer epidermis and the inner dermis. The epidermis has several layers. The cells in this top layer of skin are constantly being worn away and replaced by new cells.

Directions: Press a piece of clear tape onto the back of your hand. Pull it off. Look at the tape with a magnifying glass or under a microscope. In the box, draw what you see.

Your drawing should show the tiny flakes of dead epidermal skin. These are the cells that are continually wearing away and being replaced by new ones.

Next, use a washable marker to color your skin in two different areas—the inside of your arm and your elbow. Press both of these colored areas in the space below. Write a few sentences that describe how the skin is different in these two areas.

_____

_____

_____

_____

_____

Antibiotic Scientist

Antibiotics are drugs that fight bacteria in your body. These kinds of drugs are prescribed by a doctor. You usually take these when you are sick, but not all of the time. Antibiotics don't work against colds and the flu because these are caused by a virus, not a bacteria. Colds and the flu just have to run their courses— and you have to wait them out.

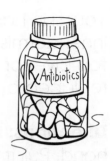

Knowing when to take antibiotics is tricky. If you take the same antibiotic too often, the bacteria can get used to the antibiotic. Then the drug won't work as well. That's why a doctor keeps track with prescriptions.

Directions: Imagine you are a scientist who develops antibiotics. A new illness is going around that does not have an antibiotic to fight it. Your job is to create a new antibiotic that will wipe out the illness. Design your antibiotic using the web below. Then write a summary on another sheet of paper that you will give to doctors to explain why they should prescribe this antibiotic.

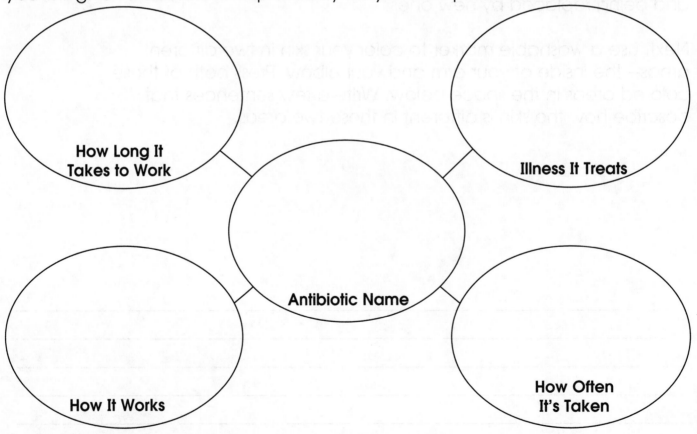

General Health Review

Directions: Answer the questions about hygiene.

1. Germs **cannot** enter your body through your
   a. nose.
   b. skin.
   c. hair.
   d. mouth.

2. Your body is made up of _____ systems that work together to keep you healthy.
   a. two
   b. four
   c. six

3. Your heart is part of your _____ system.
   a. respiratory
   b. circulatory
   c. digestive

4. Which bodily system makes your body move?
   a. circulatory
   b. digestive
   c. muscular

5. Write a summary about things you can do to keep yourself free of germs and illness. Use complete sentences. _____

   _____

   _____

   _____

6. How does hand washing keep you healthy?

   _____

   _____

Your Dental Hygiene

Ask the following questions to your students to test their animal dental knowledge.

How many more teeth do you have than an anteater? (anteaters don't have any teeth)

How many teeth would you have if you combined the teeth of a gopher, a rat, and a porcupine? (60; they each have about 20 teeth)

Deer have about 30 teeth. Do you have more teeth than a deer?

A crocodile has 60 teeth. How many babies, with all of their baby teeth, would you need to have about the same number of teeth? (3; babies have 20 baby teeth)

On the board, create a classroom KWL chart about dental hygiene. Have students record the KWL on paper so they can return to the chart after studying dental hygiene. Then they can fill in the L section of the chart.

What I Know	What I Want to Know	What I Learned

0-7424-2757-9 *Health, Hygiene, and Nutrition*

Name _____ Date _____

Visiting Dr. Bicuspid

Directions: Do you look forward to your visits to the dentist? Some people like going to the dentist, while others dread it. Write a story about one child's adventure of going to the dentist. Use the story map below to help you get started. Then use the information to write your story on another piece of paper.

Story Map

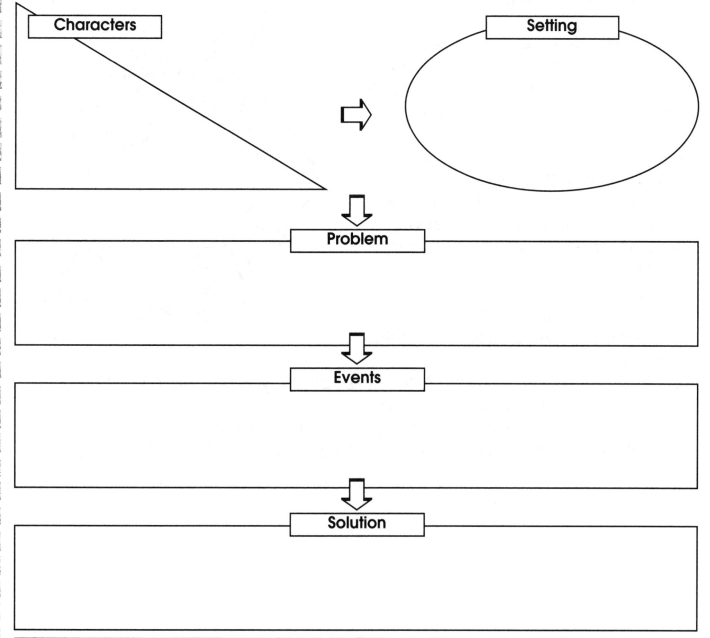

Brush Away the Plaque

Materials Needed:
one toothbrush per student, toothpaste, plaque
disclosing tablets (available at pharmacies)

Even though you brush regularly, you
may have plaque building up on your
teeth. Plaque is a sticky film of bacteria
that forms on your teeth.

Directions: Take a close look at your
teeth after you brush them. Do you
think the brushing will eliminate all the
plaque? Follow the steps below.

A. Begin by having a snack of peanut
butter and crackers.
B. Next, brush your teeth. Brush them
until you think they are clean.
C. Next, chew a plaque disclosing
tablet.
D. While looking in a mirror, count the
number of teeth that are not
clean. They will appear red. Write
down this number.
E. Once everyone has completed the activity, you will make a list of these
numbers on the board as a class.
F. Use these numbers to create a graph below that shows on how many
teeth students still had plaque. Give your graph a title and labels on both
axes.

My Pearly Whites

Directions: How do your teeth get stained? What can you brush with to remove the stains? Find out by following the steps below.

A. Soak four hard-boiled eggs in dark soda or coffee overnight.

B. Create an experiment to test the effectiveness of different toothpastes and mixtures on removing stains. You can test various toothpaste brands, plain baking soda, water, milk, hydrogen peroxide, and so on.

C. List each step below. Add more steps if needed. Then conduct the experiment.

My Pearly Whites Eggs-periment

1. _____

2. _____

3. _____

4. _____

5. _____

6. _____

Answer the following questions.

1. Did you follow your experiment step by step? _____

2. Did you forget any steps when creating your experiment? If so, what are they? _____

3. What would you do differently next time? _____

_____

Name _____ Date _____

Homemade Toothpaste

Materials Needed:
baking soda, salt, glycerin, mint flavoring, food
coloring, mixing bowl and spoon, airtight container

Directions: Make a natural toothpaste
that will clean your teeth and protect
them from decay. Follow the steps
below.

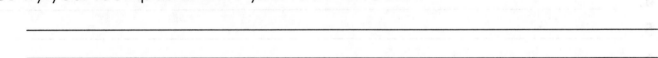

A. Mix three tablespoons of baking
   soda with one tablespoon of salt.
B. Add three teaspoons of glycerin.
C. Add 10 to 20 drops of flavoring,
   such as peppermint, wintergreen,
   or cinnamon.
D. Add one drop of food coloring.
E. Mix the ingredients thoroughly in a bowl.
F. Add water to make the mixture a similar consistency to toothpaste.
G. Try your toothpaste. Write your reaction below.

_____

_____

8. Spoon the rest of the mixture into an airtight container.

Answer the following questions.

1. What is the purpose of the baking soda? _____

2. Why should you add the flavoring? _____

3. Would toothpaste sell well if it didn't have flavoring in it?
   Why or why not?_____

0-7424-2757-9 *Health, Hygiene, and Nutrition*

Name _____ Date _____

Toothpaste Ads

Directions: Find an advertisement for toothpaste in a magazine.

What does this toothpaste claim to do?_____

What makes this toothpaste appealing or unappealing to you? _____

_____

_____

Have you ever used this toothpaste? _____

If so, did it do what it claimed to do? _____

Design an experiment that will test whether the toothpaste does what it claims to do. List the steps for the experiment below. Then conduct the experiment. Write your results below.

A Toothpaste Claim

A. _____

B. _____

C. _____

D. _____

E. _____

F. _____

Results of the experiment:

_____

_____

_____

_____

 0-7424-2757-9 *Health, Hygiene, and Nutrition*

Name _____ Date _____

A Mouth Full of Teeth

There are four basic types of teeth—molars, premolars, incisors, and canines. Each type is different and has its own job to do.

Molars

gray area on each falls below gum line

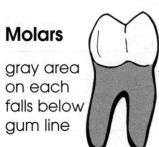

Premolars

Incisors

Canines

Directions: Choose one of the types of teeth on which to do some research. Use an encyclopedia or the Internet for your information. Use the web below on which to record the information you find. Then use this information to write your report on another piece of paper.

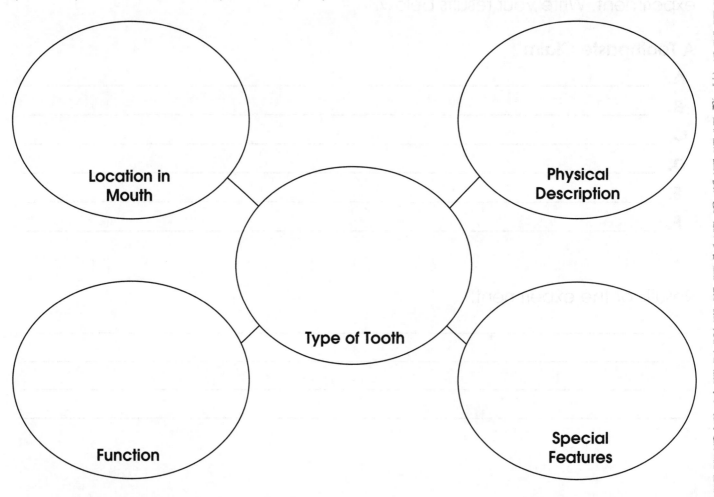

Soaperman

Directions: Create a comic strip about Soaperman. Soaperman uses his strength to wipe germs off the face of the earth.

Dental Hygiene Review

Directions: Answer the questions about dental hygiene.

1. What is plaque? _____

2. How can you get rid of plaque? _____

3. _____ can stain your teeth.
    a. milk
    b. coffee
    c. apples

4. Which of the following is not a type of tooth?
    a. canine
    b. molar
    c. dermis

5. Why is it important to practice good dental hygiene? _____
_____

6. What might happen if you neglect your teeth? _____
_____

Name _____ Date _____

Your Physical Health

Exercise is an important part of staying healthy. It helps protect you against diseases and illnesses, and it keeps your muscles and bones strong. It also helps control your weight and decrease the amount of body fat that you have.

Regular physical exercise is important for children because it helps the skeleton develop properly. Running, playing sports, and stretching are all good exercises to do. But activities such as watching TV and playing video games do not give your body the exercise it needs. These activities, when done too often, can lead to weight problems and poor physical strength.

When you exercise, it is important to eat enough calories. Your body needs energy to live and grow, and you get this energy from food. You need calories from food for basic activities of living, such as breathing, talking, walking, and sleeping. You need even more calories when you are physically active. The healthiest way to get these calories is from fruits, vegetables, meats, dairy, and grains. Exercise is also good for your mind. Exercising can improve your mood and make you feel better.

Cardiovascular Creations

Directions: In a group, brainstorm as many types of cardiovascular exercise as you can. Record these exercises below.

_____

_____

_____

_____

_____

_____

_____

Each person in your group should choose one of the exercises above and design a personal workout schedule for this activity. Write down the days on which you will do the activity and for how long. Add any other exercises or sports you do so you can see all the exercises you do for the week.

Day	Exercise or Sport	Length of Time
Sunday		
Monday		
Tuesday		
Wednesday		
Thursday		
Friday		
Saturday		

Name _____ Date _____

Stretching

Stretching is an important part of exercising. It helps loosen your muscles and prevents muscle strains and pulls.

Directions: Do the stretches below. Begin with five repetitions of each stretch, and increase the number when you are ready. Hold each stretch for 15 to 60 seconds. Do not bounce during the stretch.

Hamstring
1. Standing a foot from a wall, place your hands on the wall shoulder-height, shoulder-width apart.
2. Take a step back while pushing on the wall.
3. Keep your back straight and press your heels into the floor.
4. Hold, then step forward and repeat.

Quadriceps
1. Stand on your left leg.
2. Reach back and hold your right foot behind you with your left hand.
3. Balance against a wall with your free hand as you gently pull upward on your right foot.
4. You should feel a stretch in your right thigh but not in your knee.
5. Switch legs and repeat.

Shoulders and Back
1. Sit upright with your hands clasped behind your head.
2. Gently pull your elbows back as far as you can. Hold them in position.

Upper Body
1. Sit on the edge of your chair, firmly gripping the back.
2. Straighten your arms.
3. Keeping your back straight, let your upper body pull you forward to stretch your shoulders, upper back, and chest.

Legs
1. Sitting in a chair, grip the seat of your chair and raise one leg while you flex your foot.
2. Slowly move the leg outward, then back toward the center and down.

Intensity of Exercise

The talk test method of measuring exercise intensity is simple and can be done at any time. A person who is exercising at a low intensity level should be able to sing while doing the exercise. A person who is exercising at a moderate intensity level should be able to carry on a conversation comfortably while engaging in the exercise. A person who becomes winded or too out of breath to carry on a conversation during the exercise is exercising at too vigorous of an intensity level.

Directions: Create an experiment to rate exercise intensity using the talk test. In the space below, list the steps you will take to conduct your experiment. Then conduct your experiment by following your steps. Create a graph or chart on a separate piece of paper to show your results.

Steps

A. _____

_____

B. _____

_____

C. _____

_____

D. _____

_____

E. _____

_____

F. _____

_____

Name _____ Date _____

Taking Your Heart Rate

To get the most benefit during exercise, your heart rate should fall between 60 percent and 80 percent of its maximum capacity for at least 15 minutes. This is your target heart rate. To calculate your target heart rate:

> Subtract your age from 220 = _____
> Multiply that number by 60% for your minimum heart rate.
> Multiply that same number by 80% for your maximum heart rate.
> My target heart rate is from _____ to _____ .

Directions: Do some of the exercises below. Take the talk test to determine the intensity of the exercise for you. Then stop the exercise and take your pulse for ten seconds. Multiply this by six to calculate your heart rate during the exercise. Which exercises put your heart rate in the target zone?

Light-Intensity Exercises	Moderate-Intensity Exercises	Vigorous-Intensity Exercises
• Walking slowly • Swimming, treading slowly • Bicycling, very light effort • Doing conditioning exercise, lightly stretching or warming up	• Walking briskly • Swimming, recreational • Playing tennis, doubles • Bicycling five to nine mph on level terrain or with a few hills • Lifting weights, Nautilus® machines, or free weights	• Speed walking, jogging, or running • Swimming laps • Playing tennis, singles • Bicycling more than ten mph or on steep uphill terrain • Doing circuit training

0-7424-2757-9 *Health, Hygiene, and Nutrition*

The Flexibility Test

Do you think you are flexible? Can your body bend into all sorts of positions? The ability to move your joints freely and without pain through a wide range of motion is called flexibility. Some people are naturally more flexible than others.

Directions: Do a stretch that helps strengthen and flex your leg muscles.

A. Place a yardstick on the floor with the zero mark closest to you. Tape the yardstick to the floor at the 15-inch mark.

B. March slowly in place. Slowly increase your pace until you feel yourself heating up.

C. Sit next to the yardstick with your heels at the 15-inch mark. Your legs should be straight.

D. Place your hands on top of each other.

E. Slowly stretch forward, sliding your fingertips along the yardstick as far as you can. Do not bounce while doing this. Look at the yardstick. In the chart below, write down how far your hands reached (in inches).

F. Sit up straight and repeat the stretch. Record the distance in inches again in the chart.

G. Do this five times, resting and breathing between each stretch.

Stretch	Distance in Inches
1	_____
2	_____
3	_____
4	_____
5	_____

Answer the following questions.

1. What do you notice about the distance of each stretch? _____

2. If your distance changed, why do you think this is? _____

3. What did you feel happening to your legs? _____

4. Why do you think it's important not to bounce during this stretch? _____

_____

Name _____ Date _____

The Strength Test

Directions: Perform the following exercises to test the strength of the muscles in your upper, middle, and lower body. Record your results in the chart .

Upper Body Strength Test

Use your arms to push your body up and to lower it back down. Repeat. If necessary, do the modified version of a push-up by balancing on your knees instead of your feet.

Ratings	Number
High	25
Average	15
Below average	5
Low	less than 5

Middle Body Strength Test

Lie on your back. Put your hands behind your head. Without straining your head or neck, pull your body to a 45-degree angle. Hold for as long as you can. Return to flat position on your back. Repeat.

Ratings	Number
High	25
Average	15
Below average	5
Low	less than 5

Lower Body Strength Test

Lean back against a wall. Be sure your back is flat. Slide down the wall so your knees are at a 90-degree angle. Hold this position for as long as you can. Do this one time and time yourself.

Ratings	Seconds
High	90
Average	60
Below average	30
Low	less than 30

Body Part	High	Average	Below Average	Low
Upper				
Middle				
Lower				

Name _____ Date _____

Repetitions Graphing

Directions: Pick three exercises that you can do in the classroom, such as jumping jacks, knee squats, knee lifts, overhead book lifts, push-ups, and sit-ups.

For each exercise, you will graph your progress of doing the exercise over the course of three days. Be sure to warm up and stretch before beginning each time. Allow a day between exercises for your muscles to repair themselves. Record the number of repetitions for each exercise. Then create a graph below that shows your progress for each exercise. Label each axis and give your graph a name. Write a short summary explaining what your graph shows.

ABC Fitness Fun

Give each student two index cards. Have students write a physical activity that can be done in a short amount of time, such as *do a jumping jack for each year you have lived or do push-ups to total your favorite number.*

Collect the cards and have one person write each letter of the alphabet on the back of each card so every card is assigned a letter. Once a day, have students draw cards according to a theme you provide. For example, have students draw cards that spell their name. Then they flip over the cards and perform the exercises. Do this using the themes below, or create new ones for more exercise fun.

Exercise Card Themes

- Spell your first and last name with the cards.
- Spell your favorite exercise with the cards.
- Spell your favorite book title with the cards.
- Choose the initials of your favorite author with the cards.
- Spell your favorite color with the cards.
- Spell a word you have recently learned with the cards.
- Spell the month you were born with the cards.

Fitness Charades

Directions: Use the cards below for any of the following activities:

- With a partner, cut out the cards. Each card shows a physical activity. Turn them face down. Take turns picking a card and acting out the activity without the use of words or sounds. Have your partner try to guess what activity you are acting out.
- Sort the cards in order of the activities that burn the fewest calories to the most calories.
- Sort the cards into two groups—sports you would like to try and sports you would not like to try.
- Sort the cards into individual and group activities.
- Sort the cards by the weather or season in which they take place.

Name the Game

Directions: Create a physical game of your own where you design the rules, the number of players and teams, and so on. Give the game a name. As you develop the game, make your notes in the flowchart below. Then try to put your game to work to see if you included all the important steps, rules, directions, and so on.

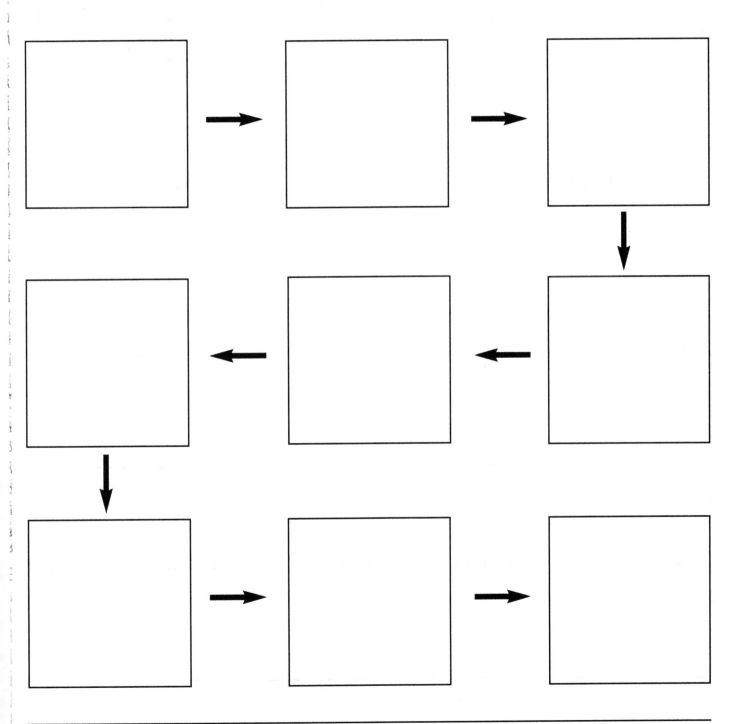

Ask the Expert

Directions: Interview a physical education teacher or a coach about the importance of exercise in total health. Have your questions ready ahead of time so you know what you want to learn from the interview. Use the form below on which to record your interview questions and answers. Then write a summary of what you learned from the interview.

Person Interviewed: _____ **Date:** _____

Questions	Responses

Name _____ Date _____

My Favorite Exercise

Directions: Fill out the graphic planner below about one of your favorite exercises. Then use this information to write a report that you will share with the class about the exercise.

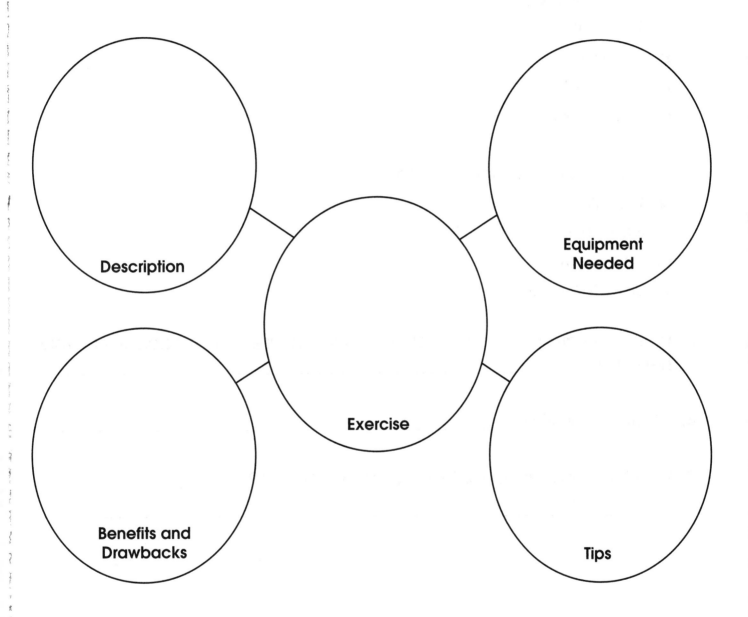

Description

Equipment
Needed

Exercise

Benefits and
Drawbacks

Tips

85

0-7424-2757-9 *Health, Hygiene, and Nutrition*

Physical Fitness Review

Directions: Answer the questions about physical fitness.

1. You should give your muscles _____ between exercising to repair themselves.
   - **a.** 20 minutes
   - **b.** one day
   - **c.** one week
   - **d.** two weeks

2. When you exercise, it is important to
   - **a.** stretch.
   - **b.** warm up.
   - **c.** cool down.
   - **d.** all of the above

3. When you are performing high-intensity exercises, what happens to your heart rate? _____

4. What is flexibility? _____

5. Why is exercise important to your overall health? _____

   _____

Exercising Your Mind

Everyone has good days and bad days. People's emotions can vary greatly from minute to minute and day to day. Humans have the ability to experience a range of emotions, such as joy, sadness, confusion, anger, and nervousness.

Directions: Draw a picture to show the emotion you are feeling right now. Then write about the emotion below.

```


```

1. My emotion is _____.

2. This emotion sounds like _____.

3. This emotion feels like _____.

4. I feel this way right now because _____.

5. If this emotion were an animal, it would be a _____.

6. When I feel this way, I like to _____.

7. Write what you like to do when you feel the following emotions:

   a. anger _____

   b. sadness _____

   c. excitement _____

   d. confusion _____

   e. anxiety _____

Name _____ Date _____

An Ideal Friend

What makes a good friend? Having good friends is important because they can influence you. If you have friends who don't pressure you but instead accept you and help you work to be your best, you will be much better off when faced with challenging issues.

Directions: Think of qualities that make a good friend. What qualities do some of your good friends have? What do you look for when choosing a friend? On the friendship map at the left, write some of these important qualities. Then use these notes to write a paper on friendship. Some things to consider are how a friend can cheer you up, how a friend can support you, how a friend can show you she cares, and so on.

Name _____ Date _____

The Stress Factor

What is stress to you? What has caused stress in your life? How do you deal with stress?

Directions: Complete the subject box below about stress. Then, in a group, pick a stressful situation from someone's subject box. Discuss how the person could overcome the stress from the situation and make the situation more pleasant. Write your notes below and be prepared to share them with the class.

Definition

Stressful Situation I Remember

Stress

Ways to Deal with Stress

Situations Where I Might Feel Stress

Situation: _____

Reasons for stress: _____

How to overcome the stress: _____

The Pressure Is On

In your life, sometimes you feel pressured to do things even though you know they are wrong and they may harm you or others. When you feel this pressure from other people of the same age, it is called peer pressure.

To demonstrate the effects of peer pressure with your students, do the following activity.

A. Speak privately with two children in your class the day before this activity. Explain to them that you want to simulate a peer-pressure scenario and the feelings that may accompany it.

B. Tell them you will have a bag of candy in the classroom the day of the activity.

C. Tell the two students that you will be called outside the classroom for a short time. Instruct them to eat some of the candy and encourage others to do the same. In other words, you want these students to try to pressure the rest of the class into eating your candy. Talk with the two students about ways to pressure the rest of the class into doing this.

D. After you have returned to the room, discuss the activity with your class and ask the following questions.
  • Did you feel pressure to take some of the candy?
  • How did the situation make you feel?
  • f you took some candy, did you regret doing so?
  • If you did not take any candy, how did you resist the pressure?
  • What are other situations in your life where you have felt pressure?

Ask your students to rate the level of peer pressure they felt on the scale below.

Friendly   Teasing   Indirect   Heavy

Name _____ Date _____

Coping with Situations at School

Directions: Recall a conflict you have had at school. What did you do about it? Was it resolved? Would you react the same if it happened again? Complete the conflict web below about the situation. Then use these notes to write a summary of the situation on another sheet of paper.

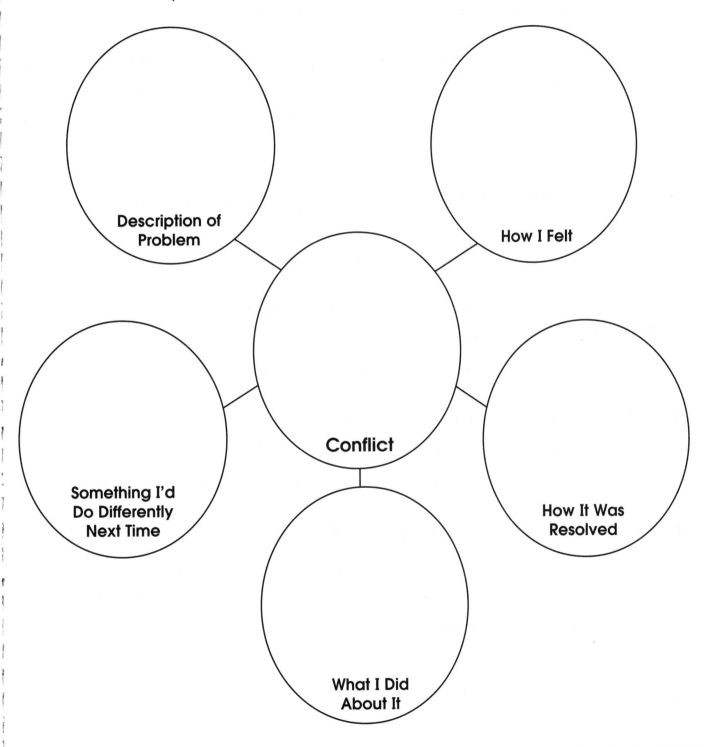

Description of Problem

How I Felt

Something I'd Do Differently Next Time

Conflict

How It Was Resolved

What I Did About It

91

0-7424-2757-9 *Health, Hygiene, and Nutrition*

Name _____ Date _____

Mental Health Review

Directions: Answer the questions about mental health.

I. What are examples of emotions that people feel?

_____

2. What are some coping strategies you can use to deal with the different emotions that you feel? _____

_____

_____

3. What qualities make a good friend? _____

_____

_____

4. Why is it important to be surrounded by people who support you rather than boss you around? _____

_____

5. What are some things you can do to be a good friend?

_____

_____

6. Write about a time when a friend did something nice for you.

_____

_____

_____

0-7424-2757-9 *Health, Hygiene, and Nutrition*

Keeping Yourself Safe

Your students are confronted often with safety issues. These safety issues can range from spoiled food to drugs to fire safety. Giving students the knowledge of how to deal with these situations is the best way to help keep them safe.

Talk to your students about things that can threaten their safety. Brainstorm a list of possible threats, and write them on the board. Then talk about ways students can avoid these threats or things students should know about these threats to protect themselves. If time permits, role-play some of the situations to show how children can keep themselves safe from danger.

Threat	How to Avoid the Threat
Drugs	Know how to say NO!
Fire	Don't play with matches or candles.
Poisoning	Have a fire extinguisher in the house.
	Know what substance is in a bottle.

Name _____ Date _____

Just Avoid It

There are two types of drugs—drugs that help you and drugs that harm you. One way to stay safe is by knowing which drugs help and which drugs harm.

A drug is any nonfood item that changes the way your body works. Some drugs are medicines. They may be helpful in preventing or treating an illness. But some drugs are not medicines, such as tobacco and alcohol. They have no medical purpose and can change the way the mind and body work. These are dangerous to take, and you should avoid them.

Directions: Read the situations below. Each one presents a risk. Write the risk it presents. Then write a possible way to avoid the risk.

Situation 1   You find some medicine sitting on the kitchen table in your house.

Risk: _____

How to avoid the risk: _____

Situation 2   You feel pressure from an older friend to use drugs.

Risk: _____

How to avoid the risk: _____

Situation 3   Your older sister smokes and wants you to try it.

Risk: _____

How to avoid the risk: _____

Situation 4   You have a headache and need a pill but aren't sure which bottle to open from the medicine cabinet. You can't read the labels.

Risk: _____

How to avoid the risk: _____

0-7424-2757-9 *Health, Hygiene, and Nutrition*

Name _____ Date _____

Looks Can Be Deceiving

Materials Needed:
clear containers of harmful liquids (medicines or cleaners) and drinks (soda, sports drinks), pills, candy pieces

Many items in your house might look like food or drink but are in fact harmful substances if swallowed.

Directions: Look at the unlabeled containers in front of you. Do not smell or taste them. Sort the items into two groups—medicines/cleaners and food/drink. Write the description of each item in the correct column below.

Medicines/Cleaners	Food/Drink

Even if you are given a drug by a doctor, you must be careful when taking it. Make a list of safety practices to use when taking any drug.

1. _____

2. _____

3. _____

4. _____

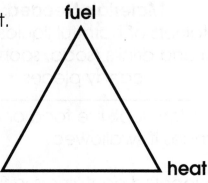

Name _____ Date _____

Fuel for the Fire

Fires need three things to burn—fuel, oxygen, and heat. These three things make up the fire triangle.

Directions: See what happens when each element of fire is removed one at a time. The teacher will light three candles. Watch as the teacher manipulates the fuel, oxygen, and heat surrounding the candle. Then draw what happens to each candle. First, draw the candle burning.

Observe as the teacher sprays the first candle with water to eliminate the heat. Draw the candle.

Observe as the second candle is covered with a glass jar. This eliminates the oxygen from the fire. The candle runs out of oxygen. Draw the candle.

Observe the third candle burn down to the bottom of the wax. This wax is the fuel, and the fuel has run out. Draw the candle.

Answer the following questions.

1. Taking away which element of fire extinguished the fire the fastest?

_____

2. What did you learn about fire from this experiment? _____

_____

Fire Extinguisher

Conduct the following experiment with your students to show what happens when oxygen is eliminated from a fire. Have them observe what you are doing and draw what they see happening. This experiment will help simulate the effects a fire extinguisher has on a fire. Fire extinguishers work by removing one of the three elements in the fire triangle— oxygen. When one of the elements is removed, the fire cannot continue burning.

A. Fill a clear, small bowl with baking soda.
B. Place an upright candle inside the bowl. Light the candle.
C. Pour vinegar on the baking soda around the candle. Be careful not to get any vinegar on the candle.
D. Place another clear bowl upside down over the bowl and candle. It should completely cover the smaller bowl and candle.
E. Have students observe what is happening inside the bowls.
F. Explain that the vinegar and baking soda mix together to produce carbon dioxide.

Discuss the following questions.
1. Why did the flame go out?
2. What element of fire was eliminated during this experiment?
3. Did the flame extinguish slowly or quickly? Why do you think this is?
4. What would happen if the top bowl did not completely cover the bottom bowl?

First Aid Kits

What should be in a first aid kit? What would you need if you got a cut, sprained your ankle, or got something in your eye? A first aid kit has many uses, so it needs to hold many useful items.

Directions: Design your own first aid kit with a partner. Think about different reasons you need to use a first aid kit. Then think about the items you need for these reasons. List each item in the first aid kit below, along with a reason for including the item. When your list is complete, look it over and choose the three most important items in the kit. Put a star by each of these items.

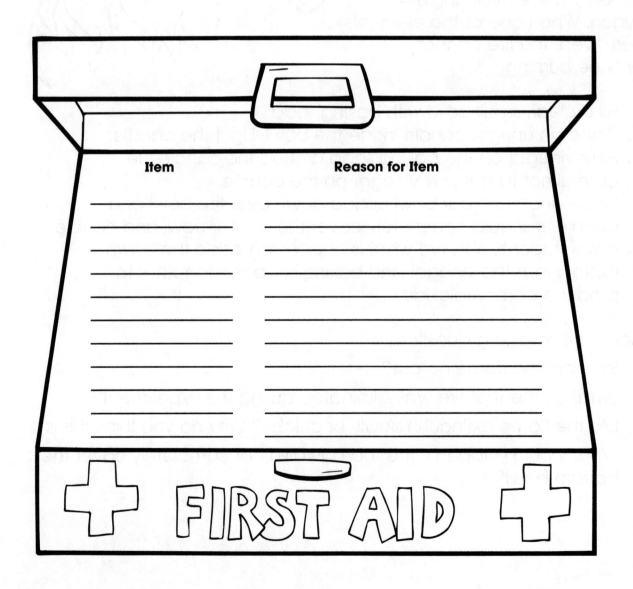

Item	Reason for Item

Name _____ Date _____

Safety Situations

Directions: For each of the situations below, think of the best approach to help the injured person. In the space provided, write how you would help the person.

1. A friend falls off her bike while riding home from school with you.

_____

2. During recess, a boy falls on the cement and scrapes his knee and elbow. _____

3. A boy falls off a swing and bumps his head on the ground.

_____

4. A friend of yours has sand in her eyes, and she can't see.

_____

5. A girl is running and falls into a shallow hole. She thinks she sprained her ankle. _____

0-7424-2757-9 *Health, Hygiene, and Nutrition*

Food Safety

> **Materials Needed:**
> eggs, small cooking pans, water,
> a heating source

Children need to be aware of food safety. Undercooked foods and spoiled foods can make them sick. Do the following activity with your students to show the importance of fully cooking food. This activity can be done as a class, in groups, or by individual students.

A. Boil the first egg for 2 minutes. Cool under cold water.

B. Boil the second egg for 8 minutes. Cool under cold water.

C. Boil the third egg for 15 minutes. Cool under cold water.

D. Compare all three eggs. How do they look and feel different from each other? Record your observations in a chart like the chart below.

E. Peel the shell off each egg. Peel the white off each egg. How are the yolks and whites different in each egg? Write your observations in the chart.

Egg	Look	Feel	Inside of Egg
Boiled for 2 min.			
Boiled for 8 min.			
Boiled for 15 min.			

Discuss the following questions.

1. Of the three eggs, which egg would you want to eat? Why?

2. Which egg might make you sick? Why?

0-7424-2757-9 *Health, Hygiene, and Nutrition*

Name _____ Date _____

Just Chill

Materials Needed per Group (3-4 students):
dry yeast packet, 1 cup of water, 1 tsp of sugar,
2 beakers, 2 balloons, 2 large bowls, thermometer

Directions: Does chilling food stop the growth of
bacteria? Do an experiment to find out.

A. In your group, mix one packet of active dry yeast
with one cup of room-temperature water and one
teaspoon of sugar. Dissolve the yeast completely.

B. Pour half the mixture into one beaker. Cover the
opening of the beaker with a balloon.

C. Pour the other half of the mixture into a second beaker.
Cover the opening of the beaker with the balloon.

D. Place the first beaker in the bowl of cold water—about 40 degrees.

E. Place the second beaker in the bowl of warm water—about 110
degrees.

F. Observe the two beakers. Write your observations below.

After 1 minute _____

_____

After 5 minutes _____

_____

After 30 minutes _____

_____

After 60 minutes _____

_____

What conclusions can you reach from this experiment? Does bacteria grow
better in cold or warm places? _____

_____

_____

0-7424-2757-9 *Health, Hygiene, and Nutrition*

Name _____ Date _____

Home Safety Assessment

Directions: How safe is your home? Are there things you can do to make your home a safer place? Assess the safety of your home. Check *yes* or *no* for all of the items below that apply. Get help from a parent, if necessary. Then review your list. What safety rating would you give your home?

	Yes	No
Safety Devices		
Smoke alarms	____	____
Carbon monoxide detectors	____	____
Circuit breakers	____	____
Fire extinguishers	____	____
Hazards		
Loose carpet or rugs	____	____
Cracked plugs	____	____
Worn electrical cables	____	____
More than one kitchen appliance on the same outlet	____	____
Knives out in the open in the kitchen	____	____
Thermostat for water set too high (hot)	____	____
Kitchen Safety		
Adult supervises cooking	____	____
Pot handles are turned inward on the stove	____	____
Fire extinguisher is within reach in the kitchen area	____	____
Towels, pot holders, and other flammable materials are kept away from the stove area	____	____
Foods are kept refrigerated until they will be used	____	____
Foods are cooked thoroughly	____	____
Surfaces are cleaned after meats and other perishable items have been used on them	____	____
Childproofing for Houses with Young Children		
Stair gates	____	____
Electrical outlet guards	____	____
Window locks	____	____
Toilet locks	____	____
Cabinet locks	____	____
Chemicals out of reach	____	____
Medicine in child-resistant containers and out of reach	____	____

A Poster for Safety

Directions: What comes to mind when you think of staying safe? Create a poster that displays ways children can keep themselves safe. Use words, drawings, and pictures from magazines to show this.

A True Safety Story

Everyone has had a scary experience where he or she was in a situation that was harmful or unsafe.

Directions: Think of an experience that happened to you or someone in your family. Complete the story map below about the situation. Fill in as much as you can. Then use these notes to write about the situation on another piece of paper.

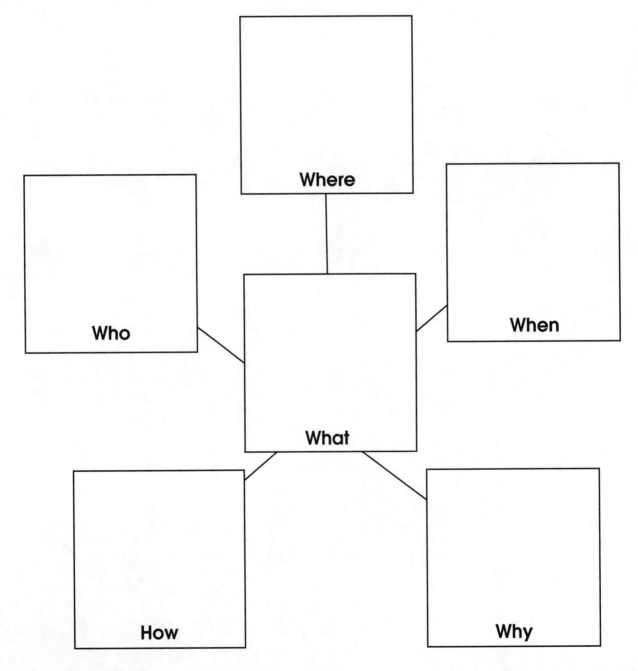

Name _____ Date _____

Choices and Consequences

People make choices every day. Some choices are easy to make, such as what to wear. Other choices are much more difficult.

Directions: Look at each choice below. Write a possible consequence for each one.

Choice	Consequence
Trying an illegal drug	
Drinking alcohol	
Riding a bike without a helmet	
Not looking before crossing the street	
Leaving a burning candle unattended	
Tasting an unknown substance	
Letting your little brother play with matches	
Smoking a cigarette	
Hanging out with people who pressure you to do bad things	
Taking a pill from an unlabeled bottle	

0-7424-2757-9 *Health, Hygiene, and Nutrition*

Name _____ Date _____

Smoking

Smoking cigarettes is a bad habit. Yet it is hard for many people to quit. Cigarette smoke affects your body in many unhealthy ways.

- Inhaling cigarette smoke reduces the amount of oxygen in your bloodstream.
- Smoking increases your heart rate because your heart must work harder to get oxygen to the rest of your body.
- Nicotine, a chemical found in tobacco, makes your blood vessels shrink. This makes your heart work harder to pump blood through your body.
- The tar found in tobacco sticks to the insides of your lungs, causing cancer in your lungs.
- Cigarette smoke contains more than 40 carcinogens, or chemicals that cause cancer.
- Cigarettes cause your skin to age faster than normal. You will have wrinkles and old-looking skin.

Directions: Interview a family member or friend about smoking. Use the following questions and create some of your own. Use a separate sheet of paper on which to record your interview. Then write a brief summary of the interview and your thoughts on smoking.

1. Why do you smoke/not smoke?

2. What do you think of other people who smoke?

3. Can you tell me what smoking does to the body?

4. Are you ever affected by secondhand smoke?

5. If you smoke, why did you start smoking? How old were you? Have you ever tried to quit?

0-7424-2757-9 *Health, Hygiene, and Nutrition*

Name _____ Date _____

Take a Deep Breath

You breathe by moving air in and out of the lungs. Breathing consists of two phases—inspiration (inhaling) and expiration (exhaling). During inspiration, the diaphragm contracts and moves downward. This enlarges your chest cavity. During expiration, the diaphragm relaxes. This decreases the size of the chest cavity.

Breathe in and out. Look down at your chest as you take a big breath, hold it, and then release it. Do you see your chest rising and falling?

Directions: Answer the following questions about how your lungs and diaphragm work.

1. What happens to your lungs and diaphragm as you inhale?

_____

_____

2. What happens to your lungs and diaphragm as you exhale?

_____

_____

3. What are some things that can affect your breathing?

_____

_____

 0-7424-2757-9 *Health, Hygiene, and Nutrition*

The Effects of Smoking

The tobacco from cigarettes produces a brown, sticky tar that coats the insides of lungs of people who smoke. Over time, this has a harmful effect on the lungs, causing them not to work they way they should. Tobacco in cigarettes can cause diseases such as lung cancer, emphysema, and asthma. Smoking cigarettes can even cause death.

Directions: To simulate the effects of smoking on lungs, do the following experiment.

A. Get a large balloon. This represents a lung that has not been exposed to smoke. Blow into the balloon. Release the air from the balloon. Repeat. This is how the air you breathe enters and exits your lungs.

B. Into a second balloon, squirt two teaspoons of glue.

C. Let it dry overnight. This represents the lung of a smoker with deposits of tar from cigarettes.

D. After the balloon is dry, repeat the steps you followed with the first balloon. Blow into the balloon and release the air. Repeat several times. What difference do you notice from the first balloon?

Summarize what this experiment shows about the effects of smoking on a person's lungs. _____

_____

_____

_____

_____

Name _____ Date _____

Do You Smell Smoke?

Secondhand smoke is just as harmful to you as firsthand smoke. Secondhand smoke occurs when you inhale another person's cigarette smoke that is floating in the air around you. Sometimes secondhand smoke is hard to avoid. Many public places, such as malls, restaurants, and airplanes, have banned cigarette smoking. However, you may still find yourself in places where people smoke.

Directions: In the space below, create a billboard to convince lawmakers to ban smoking in ALL public places. Use words, pictures, drawings, and anything else you think will help make your point.

Alcohol Is Addictive

Alcohol is a type of drug called a depressant. It slows down your reaction time and may make you do things you wouldn't normally do. Both of these effects can be dangerous. Alcohol is a drug that can be very addictive. This means that it is hard for people to quit. That's why it is important never to start using alcohol. Alcohol usage over time can have serious health effects.

Directions: As a class, brainstorm a list of harmful things that can happen as a result of using alcohol. Write your list below.

Harmful Situations Caused by Using Alcohol

Drunk Driving Simulation

To simulate the effects of alcohol on motor skills, do the following activity with your students.

Choose a student to stand in the center of an open area clear of desks, walls, bookshelves, and so on. Choose two or three students to stand around the student in the center. These students will spin the student for 30 seconds in a clockwise direction. After 30 seconds of
spinning, have the student attempt some of the following activities to test his or her fine and gross motor skills. Repeat the activity with different students in the center. For safety reasons, make sure the student in the center is surrounded by other students while doing the activities.

- Walk a straight line
- Write his or her name straight across on the board
- Draw a straight line on the board
- Pour a glass of water
- Dribble a ball
- Cut out a pattern from paper (use dull scissors for safety reasons)
- Pin a magnetic item on a bull's-eye
- Color a picture (in the lines)

After the activity, discuss the following questions.
1. What does this activity show about the effects of alcohol on your motor skills?
2. How might you feel behind the wheel of a car after drinking alcohol?
3. How did you feel after being spun in a circle for 30 seconds? Was this a good feeling?
4. Did you feel in control of your body?
5. What did you learn about the way alcohol can affect your body and mind?

Name _____ Date _____

The Cycle of Addiction

People can easily become addicted to drugs. At first, people feel good when taking a drug. But the drug use slowly starts to destroy friendships, family relationships, self-esteem, and confidence. The person using the drug ends up feeling alone and depressed. Drugs are very dangerous.

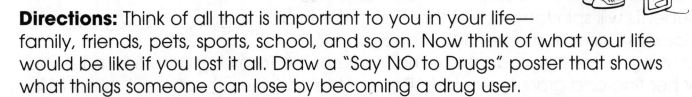

Directions: Think of all that is important to you in your life—family, friends, pets, sports, school, and so on. Now think of what your life would be like if you lost it all. Draw a "Say NO to Drugs" poster that shows what things someone can lose by becoming a drug user.

0-7424-2757-9 *Health, Hygiene, and Nutrition*

Magazine Messages

Directions: Look through magazines for advertisements of cigarettes and alcohol. Cut out the advertisements and use them to create a collage on construction paper.

After you have created your collage, look at the pictures. What are the messages that the advertisements are trying to send? After what you've learned about cigarettes and alcohol, are the advertisements accurate?

_____

_____

What do you notice about how cigarettes and alcohol are portrayed?

_____

_____

Now create your own ad that gives a true picture of the effects of cigarettes and alcohol. Use the space below.

Safety Review

Directions: Answer the questions about safety.

1. A first aid kit is useless when someone gets hurt.   **True   False**

2. A fire cannot burn without _____, _____, and _____.

3. Fire extinguishers eliminate which element from the fire triangle?

    a. oxygen

    b. fuel

    c. heat

    d. light

4. Which of the following is **NOT** something that will help keep you and your family safe?

    a. Adults should supervise during cooking activities.

    b. Children can do anything they want in the house.

    c. Outlet plugs should be covered if young children are in the house.

    d. Smoke detectors should be present.

5. List three things you learned about safety.

    a. _____

    b. _____

    c. _____

6. In what ways can a drug affect your body and mind?

_____

_____

_____

Name _____ Date _____

They All Matter

Directions: What does it mean to keep yourself healthy? Reflect on everything you have learned about nutrition, exercise, safety, health, and friendship. How do all of these factors in your life work together to keep you healthy? Write an essay below to explain this.

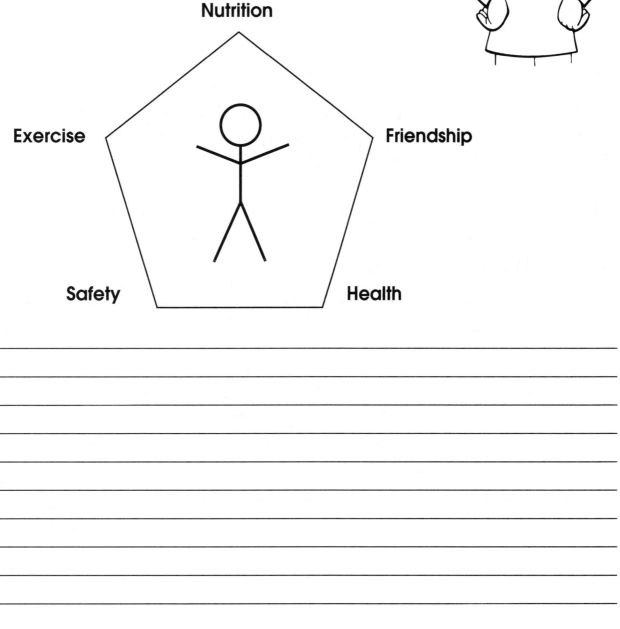

Nutrition

Exercise

Friendship

Safety

Health

_____

_____

_____

_____

_____

_____

_____

_____

_____

_____

Still Wondering

You've learned a lot about how to be as healthy as possible.
However, you may have thought of questions that did not get answered.

Directions: List some questions that you still have about health, hygiene, and nutrition.

1. _____
2. _____
3. _____
4. _____

Choose a question from above on which to do some research.
Use an encyclopedia, the library, or the Internet to search for
information to help you answer this question.

Question: _____

Sources of information: _____
_____
_____
_____

Answer: _____
_____
_____
_____

Give One, Get One

You probably remember things about health, hygiene, and nutrition that other students forgot, and vice versa. Play Give One, Get One to refresh your memory and the memories of your classmates.

Directions: Write ten things in the Give One column below that you learned about health, hygiene, and nutrition. When you finished, wander around the room and trade facts with other students. If another student tells you something he or she learned that you didn't write down, write it in the Get One column. The other student can do the same with your facts.

Give One	Get One

117

Name _____ Date _____

Healthy Acrostic Poem

Directions: Write an acrostic poem about something you learned about your health and safety. Write the word, such as *exercise*, *diet*, *caution*, or *drugs*, down the left side of the page in large letters. Then write your words or phrases for each letter going across the page.

Flavorful
Ripe
Unusual shapes
I love them!
Tangerines are my favorite.
Sweet

0-7424-2757-9 *Health, Hygiene, and Nutrition*

Name _____ Date _____

Feed Yourself Well

Directions: Using what you have learned about nutrition and the food pyramid, create a menu for yourself for a week's worth of meals.

Day	Breakfast	Lunch	Dinner
Sunday			
Monday			
Tuesday			
Wednesday			
Thursday			
Friday			
Saturday			

0-7424-2757-9 *Health, Hygiene, and Nutrition*

Name _____ Date _____

Destination: Digestive System

Directions: You are a piece of food. Maybe you're a piece of pizza, a bite of an apple, or a piece of gum that is accidentally swallowed. Write a story about your adventure through the digestive system using what you have learned. Use dialogue, humor, and descriptive words to make your story come to life. Before you write your story, jot down your ideas below. Create your own graphic planner. It can be a flowchart, a story map, an idea web, or something unique that you create to help you plan your story. Write your story on another piece of paper.

A Scrambled Story

Directions: Write a story about cleanliness using all the words in the Word Bank. Compare your story to a classmate's story to see how similar or different they are.

Word Bank			
sneeze	laughed	crowd	doorknob
breeze	truck	Aunt Betty	school play
grocery store	slipped		

_____

_____

_____

_____

_____

_____

_____

_____

_____

_____

_____

_____

_____

_____

_____

_____

_____

_____

_____

_____

_____

_____

A Haiku by You

Directions: Create a haiku on a topic you have learned about in health, hygiene, and nutrition. It can be about hand washing, peer pressure, fruits and vegetables, cigarettes, types of teeth, or another topic that you enjoyed learning about. A haiku is a type of poem that has three lines that don't rhyme. The first and third lines have five syllables each. The middle line has seven syllables. Look at the following example.

Fruits, vegetables, meat
All important to my diet
Keep me feeling good

Now create your own haiku.

_____

_____

_____

Name _____ Date _____

Peer Pressure Readers' Theater

Directions: Create a readers' theater about peer pressure using all or some of the characters below. You can add your own characters, too. After you have completed it, assign roles to friends and classmates and act it out. Use another piece of paper on which to write your script.

Evil Eddie: boy who likes to get other kids in trouble

Bashful Betty: girl who likes to make other kids happy

Tough Tommie: boy who likes to push smaller kids around

Quiet Cory: usually goes along with the crowd, regardless of the situation

Cool Carl: popular boy who does not give in to peer pressure

Confident Charlie: boy who always knows right from wrong

Mrs. Mediator: teacher

0-7424-2757-9 *Health, Hygiene, and Nutrition*

Name _____ Date _____

Connections to Standards

Nutrition

Content Standard A:
As a result of activities in grades K–4, all students should develop
- Abilities necessary to do scientific inquiry
- Understanding about scientific inquiry

Content Standard C:
As a result of activities in grades K–4, all students should develop understanding of
- The characteristics of organisms
- Life cycles of organisms

Content Standard F:
As a result of activities in grades K–4, all students should develop understanding of
- Personal health

Hygiene

Content Standard A:
As a result of activities in grades K–4, all students should develop
- Abilities necessary to do scientific inquiry
- Understanding about scientific inquiry

Content Standard F:
As a result of activities in grades K–4, all students should develop understanding of
- Personal health

Dental Hygiene

Content Standard A:
As a result of activities in grades K–4, all students should develop
- Abilities necessary to do scientific inquiry
- Understanding about scientific inquiry

Content Standard F:
As a result of activities in grades K–4, all students should develop understanding of
- Personal health

Safety

Content Standard A:
As a result of activities in grades K–4, all students should develop
- Abilities necessary to do scientific inquiry
- Understanding about scientific inquiry

Content Standard F:
As a result of activities in grades K–4, all students should develop understanding of
- Personal health

Physical Fitness

Content Standard A:
As a result of activities in grades K–4, all students should develop
- Abilities necessary to do scientific inquiry
- Understanding about scientific inquiry

Content Standard C:
As a result of activities in grades k–4, all students should develop understanding of
- The characteristics of organisms
- Life cycles of organisms

Content Standard F:
As a result of activities in grades K–4, all students should develop understanding of
- Personal health

0-7424-2757-9 *Health, Hygiene, and Nutrition*

Suggested Books for Health, Hygiene, and Nutrition

The Ultimate Sport Lead-Up Game Book: Over 170 Fun & Easy-To-Use Games To Help You Teach Children Beginning Sport Skills by Guy Bailey

Kid's Choice Cookbook by Colleen Bartley

Kid's Yoga Deck: 50 Poses and Games by Annie Buckley

The Healthy Body Cookbook: Over 50 Fun Activities and Delicious Recipes for Kids by Joan D'Amico and Karen Eich Drummond

Games to Keep Kids Moving: P.E. Activities to Promote Total Participation, Self-Esteem, and Fun for Grades 3–8 by Bob Dieden and Robert C. Dieden

Ready-to-Use P.E. Activities for Grades 3–4 by Joanne M. Landy and Maxwell J. Landy

What's Happening to My Body? Book for Girls: A Growing Up Guide for Parents and Daughters by Lynda Madaras and Area Madaras

What's Happening to My Body? Book for Boys: A Growing Up Guide for Parents and Sons by Lynda Madaras and Area Madaras

Health, Safety, and Nutrition for the Young Child by Lynn R. Marotz, Marie Z. Cross, and Jeanettia M. Rush

The Care & Keeping of You: The Body Book for Girls by Valorie Lee Schaefer

P.E. Teacher's Skill-by-Skill Activities Program: Success-Oriented Sports Experience for Grades K–8 by Lowell F. Turner

Congratulations!

This award is given to

_____

for being such a healthy person!

Way to go!

Healthy You Award!

:U

126

0-7424-2757-9 *Health, Hygiene, and Nutrition*

Nutrition Labels 17
1. 10 cookies
2. 190 calories
3. vitamin A, calcium, iron
4. 10 mg
5. two servings—20 crackers; four servings—40 crackers
6. Answers will vary.

Fruit Juice Fun 25
1. Answers will vary.
2. The juices were a darker orange color with less water. They tasted more orange-y, too.
3. sugar

The Best Selection 39
1. The wheat bread is the healthier choice. It contains less of everything that is bad for you (fat, calories, cholesterol, sugar), and it contains more fiber, which is good for you.
2. The wheat bread does not have a lot of calories, fat, sodium, or cholesterol. It also contains fiber and protein.
3. The coffee cake contains protein.
4. Answers will vary.

Nutrition Review 45
1. d
2. six
3. c
4. b
5. dairy—builds strong bones and teeth
   protein—builds strong muscles
   vegetables—gives me good eyesight
   fruits—heals cuts and bruises
   grains—gives me energy
6. Answers will vary.

They're in Your Blood 49
1. Red
2. platelets
3. white
4. 4 to 5 liters
5. You could get sick easily if your body had a low white blood cell count.
6. If your body did not have any platelets, you would bleed continuously from a cut or wound.

Germs Multiply 50
1. You could control the growth of bacteria by controlling the environment in which they thrive.
2. after five minutes—1,024 bacteria
   after ten minutes—1,048,576 bacteria

An A-Peeling Skin 60
1. Your skin prevents germs from entering your body.
2. Keeping your skin healthy and free of cuts keeps germs out of your body.
3. You can keep your cuts covered with an antibiotic ointment and a bandage.

General Health Review 63
1. c
2. b
3. b
4. c
5. Answers will vary.
6. Answers will vary.

Dental Hygiene Review 72
1. Plaque is a sticky film of bacteria that forms on teeth.
2. Brushing and flossing regularly will remove plaque.
3. b
4. c
5. Answers will vary.
6. Answers will vary.

Physical Fitness Review 86
1. b
2. d
3. It increases.
4. Flexibility is the ability to bend your body into many positions with ease.
5. Answers will vary.

Fuel for the Fire **96**
1. heat
2. Answers will vary.

Take a Deep Breath **107**
1. Your lungs fill with air and your diaphragm rises when you inhale.
2. Your lungs empty the air and your diaphragm falls when you exhale.
3. Things that can affect your breathing: smoking, cold air, asthma, vigorous exercise, quality of air

Safety Review **114**
1. false
2. oxygen, heat, and fuel
3. a
4. b
5. Answers will vary.
6. Answers will vary.